The Empowered Gal's 9 Life Lessons

Keys, Tips, Strategies, Advice & Everything You Need to Know
to be a Confident, Successful, in Control Gal

Kate Whitfield

iUniverse, Inc.
New York   Bloomington

The Empowered Gal's 9 Life Lessons
Keys, Tips, Strategies, Advice & Everything You Need to Know to be a
Confident, Successful, in Control Gal

Copyright © 2008 by Kate Whitfield

iUniverse books may be ordered through booksellers or by contacting:

iUniverse
1663 Liberty Drive
Bloomington, IN 47403
www.iuniverse.com
1-800-Authors (1-800-288-4677)

ISBN: 978-0-595-47829-3 (pbk)

Printed in the United States of America

Thank You!

It's pretty much been me and my Mac, sitting here writing these 80,719 words, but we all know it's more than just me who made this book possible. So, with great gratitude, I'd like to thank the following people:

Daddio, thanks so much for *everything*. You are the best dad and friend that anybody could ever have, and I'm so glad that I get to be your daughter. Thanks for your support, encouragement, and belief in me.

Mrs. Hutchings, my fifth-grade teacher and very first mentor, who encouraged me to write and challenge myself to be the best I could be, I'm so grateful to you and everything you have done for me. Who would have though all this started with the story of "Bilbo the Singing Goat"?

All my MySpace girls who sent in stories, quotes, ideas, feedback, and encouragement, you guys have been so helpful, right from the beginning. Thanks for being awesome!

Mark Victor Hansen, thank you for being so super-cool. Seeing you speak when I was fourteen years old changed my life, and it's the reason this book is here. Getting to meet you was such an honor, especially when you not only lived up to my mega-high expectations but exceeded them in every way.

Sam Horn, thanks for your support, encouragement, and belief in me. You are such a wonderful mentor, and I appreciate everything so much.

Everybody who supported and encouraged me throughout this process and everybody who helped me edit this book, thank you; I couldn't have done it without you. Clint, thanks for everything; I "heart" you. Goose, thank you; I love that I get to be your sister. Lynne Hannay and the Hannay family, you guys are my California family; thank you for everything. All my friends, thanks for being so understanding throughout this process and contributing stories of your own. And my puppy, Allie, thanks for never leaving my side. You are the best dog a girl could have.

Thanks in advance to all you girls who read this book and who are changing the world. You inspire me the most!

What's Inside!

Introduction

> *"Although there may be tragedy in your life, there's always a possibility to triumph. It doesn't matter who you are, [or] where you come from. The ability to triumph begins with you. Always."*
>
> —Oprah Winfrey,
> Emmy award–winning talk show host

Hey, Empowered Gals!

You are probably wondering a whole bunch of things right now, like "Thanks, Mom—another book. How am I supposed to read this *and* get my algebra homework done?" or "So, what makes this book different from all the other books I've read?" Or, you might be wondering about all the other things that teen girls wonder and worry about, like how you are supposed to fit in, make friends, keep friends, deal with gossip, feel good about your body, do well at school, get asked out on a date, be a good girlfriend, get a job, find out what you want to do for the rest of your life, stay healthy, how to make good decisions about sex, and how you are going to make your place in this world. I was just in Teenville myself a couple of years ago, so I'm no stranger to any of those questions. And I'm not going to promise you that this book will tell you the answers, because everybody's answers will be different. All this book will do is help you figure out those answers—and more—for yourself.

You might be wondering why this book is different. First of all, I'm 22, and I remember what it's like being right where you are now, and since I've been through it all, survived it, and made it out the other side, I can now pass on all the info to you. So, this isn't going to be one of those books written by some well-meaning but out-of-touch adult who wants you to "stay in school, and don't do drugs!" Sure, I want those things for you, too, but I'm coming at it from a different angle.

Being a teen girl is like riding a roller coaster, except you step on it as a kid, and you don't get off it until you are an adult.

When I was in high school, I felt alone and misunderstood, like most teens. I was the older sister, and my mom wasn't really able to "be there" for me, so I didn't have anybody to talk to who could give me advice or tell me what to expect. I wished for somebody to come along and give me tips and advice, let me know what was happening, and reassure me that everything was going to be okay, even though I felt that was the last thing that would ever happen. And now that I've "been there, done that"—survived high school, started my business, achieved things I'm really proud of, overcome some really difficult obstacles, and built a life that I'm really excited about—I feel like I can be that older, wiser best friend that *I* was looking for—for you!

This book is filled with over 1001 tips (yup, I counted!) that you can start using *today*, everything from getting real, honest-to-goodness, body-loving confidence to being a star at school, becoming a global citizen, and doing your part to change the world. This book is about action and results that you can start to see right away, because why wait any longer? When I was in high school, I wanted steps—a formula for success, stuff I could do to get closer to what I wanted *right now.* I wanted the inside scoop; I wanted to know stuff that I wasn't being told; I wanted a friend to guide me through it. I hope this book is all that—and then some—for you.

This book is for every teen who has ever complained about something in her life. Why? Because when you complain, you do so because you know there is another option, a better one, something else that you want. This book helps you get that, whatever it may be. You complain about your grades because you want better ones; you complain about things that are hard because you want them to be easier, right? What do you complain about the most? Instead of focusing on the problem, let's work on the solution. This book takes the inaction of complaining and turns it into action, moving towards more of what you want and leaving behind what you don't.

Of course, there are some things you can't change. I mean, your parents are your parents, your genes are your genes, and your location is your location. But you *can* change the relationship with your parents, you *can* do stuff to nurture the relationship with your body, and you *can* make the best of living where you live right now and work towards a future somewhere else. See? Complaining isn't that bad after all, because it shows you want you want. Now it's up to you to do something about it!

But, before we get going, we need to clear up some important things; like, what is an Empowered Gal (EG) anyway? And what on earth are those 9 Life Lessons?

First of all, an EG is a young woman who knows who she is, takes action to get what she wants, and takes responsibility for her life and her future. She knows she is fabulous and strong and can do anything she puts her mind to. Every girl can be an EG. It doesn't happen overnight, but trust that she is in there, just waiting to be let out. And with the help of this book, she will be!

The 9 Life Lessons will provide you with an intro to the nine most important areas of your life. It's like Math 101 or English 101 at school—it provides you with the basic groundwork that you build on, more and more every year, for the rest of your life. It puts you in the driver's seat. You might not be able to control the ups and downs, and you probably will encounter hills, valleys, and obstacles along the way, but you do control which roads you take and how quickly you get to different destinations. And just like life, there are different forks that lead you off in different directions, and it's up to you to decide which ones you want to take. You can take the ones that lead you closer to your dream life or farther away from it, and it's ultimately up to you where you go. The lessons in this book will help you make the right decisions for you, whatever they may be, and help you steer yourself towards a life you love—but I'm getting ahead of myself.

These 9 Life Lessons came from what I remember about being a teen and what girls all over the world are going through, right this very second. I realized that no matter where you live, whether it is the middle of farm country or the mansions of Beverly Hills, if you are a teen girl, you are going through pretty much the same stuff. How do I know? I asked you! Well, not *you* you, but girls in general. What follows are the most common responses to the age-old question: What do you really, really, really want?

"I want to actually like who I am and what I look like. I want to stop comparing myself to other girls and learn how to be okay with me and my body."
— Melissa, 14

"I want to have a good friend who I can count on. no matter what."
— Tanya, 15

"I want to have a great relationship with my mom and dad. I want to be able to communicate with them better than I do now."
— Denise, 15

"I want to have relationships with guys that aren't so dramatic. Plus. I want to understand them; they are so confusing!"
— Dominique, 18

"I want make the right choices when it comes to sex. There's so much pressure that I'm not sure what to do."
— Patty, 17

"I want to do well in school. be better at studying. and get into a really good college."
— Michelle, 16

"I want a good job. so that I can support myself and my family. That's really important to me."
— Lucinda, 18

"I want to be healthy. have energy. and do good things for my body."
— Charlotte, 16

"I want to give back and make a difference. I want to feel like I matter."
— Ryan, 15

Here's what I think: I think you want to like yourself more, get to know who you are, feel good about yourself, love your body, feel confident in your skin, have better friendships, be a better friend, deal with mean girls and peer pressure, stand up for yourself, get on better with your parents, make healthier choices about dating and sex, have the courage to decide what's right for you, get better grades, do well in school, get accepted into your dream school, make some money, find your passion, get healthy and have more energy, give back, and make a difference in the world. You, like most teens, probably just don't know how. It can be hard, I know! But now, you hold in your hands the first step in getting there. The catch is that just reading this book isn't enough; you need to turn these words into action, and apply these lessons to your own life.

By the end of this book, you will be able to:

- Identify the difference between real self-esteem and "fake" self-esteem.
- Stop playing characters in your life and start being *you*.
- Be a self-esteem queen and figure out who you are
- Banish the "body blues," and start working towards a loving, nurturing relationship with your body.
- Be media smart, and banish your self-esteem robbers.
- Identify the right friends for you, and strengthen the friendships you have.
- Survive the ups and downs of the friend-o-coaster.
- Become *you* centered, not friend or guy centered.
- Spot and deal with toxic friends and mean girls.
- Understand your parents, and work towards a win/win relationship.
- Stop pushing your parents' buttons, and get more of what you want.
- Communicate effectively to get your point across the right way.
- Figure out if you are ready to date, and who you want to date.
- Date smart, respect yourself, and get what you need from the relationship.
- Make healthy decisions about dating, and date for the right reasons.
- Deal with breakups the EG way.
- Make the right sex decisions for *you*.
- Decode guy lingo and know what he really means when he says what he says.
- Understand the importance of protecting yourself.
- Know why abstinence is awesome, and why you should wait until you are ready.
- Succeed at school, and improve your performance.

- Study smart, and deal with test stress and anxiety.
- Identify what kind of postsecondary education you want, and take steps to get there.
- Find the right job for you and get it.
- Ace every interview and become irreplaceable at work.
- Start planning now for your dream career and make it happen.
- Identify what is and isn't healthy and how to eat right and exercise the right way.
- Mind your mental health.
- Avoid addictions and resist peer pressure.
- Give back, and become socially responsible.
- Take easy steps to "green up" your life and save the planet.

And that's just the beginning! This book will transform you and the way that you think about your life. It is designed to be your BBFF (best book friend forever). It is 100 percent real, authentic, and from the heart. Whether you are deliriously happy, screaming at the top of your lungs, collapsed in a heap on your bedroom floor, feeling misunderstood, laughing uncontrollably, confused, heartbroken, upset, or a combination of the above, I can guarantee you that it gets easier—and way more fun. But that doesn't mean that you can't make the most of *right now*. Life is happening all around you, and wishing it away is such a mega-waste! You have so much awesome potential to do cool stuff, change your life, change the world, and start working towards your dreams and goals.

Even though you are probably still living at home, going to school, and dependent on your parents doesn't mean that you don't have control over your life. Take it from me—you have *way* more than you give yourself credit for. You control things like:

- The clothes you wear
- The people you hang out with
- The makeup and hairstyle you choose
- The music you listen to
- Your friends
- Your boyfriend/girlfriend
- Decisions about drugs, drinking, or breaking the law
- How you treat people
- How hard you work
- Your grades
- How you talk to people
- Your honesty and integrity

Cool, right? It's 100 percent your decision what to do about those things. It's also up to you how you use this book. You can flip through it, skim a couple chapters that interest you here and there, put it on your shelf for a lazy Sunday down the road, or give it away ... *or* you could invest in yourself, sit down, and read through it. Like everything in your life, it's up to you!

And remember it's *your* book! Use it, make notes in the margin, highlight stuff, mark the pages you want to go back to, and write answers to questions asked in the blank spaces provided. There are also note pages in the back that you can use to take notes or jot down ideas.

And case you were wondering who I am, I can start by telling who I'm not: I'm *not* the kid of a famous doctor or author; I'm *not* a therapist; I'm *not* a middle-aged man or woman who wants to get in on the teen market by writing a "Thou shall not do xyz" kind of book; I'm not a socialite, a model, or a recovering addict of any kind. I'm pretty much just like you, except in an older been-there-survived-that kind of way. I have researched, talked to thousands of teen girls, and conducted surveys, while also drawing on my own teen experiences, and in doing so, I found out what kind of book *you* wanted to read. Who else am I? I am the founder of EG Inc., a company all about *you*. I speak at high schools, events, seminars, and pretty much anywhere with a mic and young people. I am also a crazy yorkie lover. I hate to fly but do it all the time. I'm sometimes super-confused and overwhelmed. I love food, especially anything cooked by my dad. I'm a farm girl at heart. I love my life, and would one day love my own TV and/or cooking show. I have a minor addiction to reality TV. And one of my favorite things to do is collect sea glass in Santa Barbara. Oh, and the thing I'm most passionate about in the entire world is working with teen girls and helping them transform their lives and realize their awesome potential! That's me, ladies! But most important, I'm on your team. This book is sort of like a conversation between me and you, just like I would talk to you if you were sitting in my living room. I want you to use these lessons, like I did, to start creating your life your way.

Sound good? All right, let's go!

Welcome to *The Empowered Gal's 9 Life Lessons*!

xoxo
Kate
Vancouver, BC
May 6, 2008

Lesson 1:
Confident Gal 101

Confident gals know that it's not about how tall, small, cute, sexy, rich, famous, skinny, fashionable, or "it" you are; real confidence comes from inside. It means that you are able to say "I'm fine, I'm okay, and I'm good enough—because I say so!" So what you have *no* idea who you are or who you want to be? You're a teen…you're allowed to be a little confused! But, you *can* start getting to know yourself a little better, find out what makes you tick, connect to your inner goddess and banish your body blues—for good!

"We ask ourselves, 'Who am I to be brilliant, gorgeous, talented, and famous?' Actually, who are you not to be?"
—Marianne Williamson,
spiritual activist, author, founder of The Peace Alliance

I was the "smart" one growing up, and my sister was the "pretty, athletic" one. Doesn't sound too devastating, but as a twelve-year-old, I just assumed that I wasn't pretty because I was "smart" instead. I didn't get that I could be *both*. It wasn't until years later that I realized that I *was* both, and just because I didn't look like the glamazons in the magazines (who does?), that didn't mean that I couldn't embrace myself, love myself, and feel great in my skin. I was really lucky to get that "aha!" moment when I was in my early teens, because tons of us gals spend way too many years feeling bad, hating ourselves, and shrinking down and becoming less. If that sounds like you, remember that you should be spending that time growing into who you are and embracing all the lumps, bumps, curves, quirks, unique qualities, and everything else that makes you ... well, you!

Whether you call it confidence, self-esteem, or self-worth, it all refers to the same thing—loving your awesome self, making no apologies for who you are, and growing into the kind of woman you would want your daughter to be. Of course, you might not want to have kids—that's your choice, too—but assume that you do. You wouldn't want your little girl hating how she looks, feeling super-unsure of herself, telling herself she's ugly, fat or stupid, and hiding who she is to fit in with girls who don't even care about her.

You would want her to rock it! You would want her to embrace who she is, be proud of herself, and know she is worth way more than what Hollywood images would have her believe. I want the same for *you*! Before you begin your first "class," Confidence 101, let's check on your self-confidence "IQ." Just answer the following questions with a 1, 2, or 3; then add them up, and check below to see what your score says about you.

What's Your Confident Gal IQ?

1 = No way; **2** = Sorta, sometimes; **3** = Sure do!

	1	2	3
1. I feel like I know who I am.	1	2	3
2. I enjoy time by myself to reflect and think.	1	2	3
3. I have good mentors and role models who support me.	1	2	3
4. I am comfortable in my skin and my body.	1	2	3
5. I have a personal style that reflects who I am.	1	2	3
6. My friends make me feel good about myself.	1	2	3
7. I walk with my head high and shoulders back.	1	2	3
8. I try new things and step out of my comfort zone.	1	2	3
9. I usually feel good about myself and like who I am.	1	2	3
10. I have an "I can do it" attitude about life.	1	2	3

Now add up the numbers and find your **Confident Gal IQ**.   **Total:** _____

Scoring:

10-15: Okay, so you could really use a confidence makeover! But the good news is, the wait is over! It's totally normal to have insecurities and feel unsure of yourself, but it doesn't mean you are destined to a life of self-loathing. It just takes a little time, some understanding, and getting to know your inner gal, so it's totally do-able!

16-22: So, you are middle of the road in the confidence department, liking yourself some days and having "I just wanna crawl in a hole" days on others. I think you deserve better! Why not have those great days every day?

23-30: Seems like you have that confidence thing down pat, but that doesn't mean you don't still have the odd bout of body blues and wish there were one or two things you could change about yourself. The cool thing is you can make peace with yourself—totally, madly, and deeply.

In "What Is Self-Esteem, Anyway?" you'll learn that high self-esteem • a good body image = confidence. You'll also find out how to tell real self-esteem from "fake" self-esteem and how to tell if you are the real "you" or just playing a character, and you'll learn about real girls and their insecurities. In "Be a Self-Esteem Queen," you'll learn how to become confident from the inside out and start being an "actionista" by taking steps to feel really super awesome about yourself. In the last section, "Bodacious Body-Loving Gal," you'll learn why girls have such a hard time with their bodies and how to start developing a loving, healthy relationship with yours.

What Is Self-Esteem, Anyway?

"To me, having good self-esteem means being sure of yourself, knowing who you are, and wanting to be more of what you are capable of."
— Joni, 21

"Self-esteem is standing up for yourself and what you believe in—all the time, no matter who you are with."
— Rebecca, 18

"It makes me sad to see the girls at my school. They try so hard to be grown up and make people believe they have confidence, but a lot of times they are mean to people, always try to bring people down, and make really bad choices when it comes to guys. I don't think that's true [self-esteem] at all."
— Sam, 17

Does self-esteem come from fitting in with what society tells us is beautiful? Do we really have to live up to other people's expectations, buy "it" items, and conform to the idea that big boobs, a tiny waist, long legs, a super-orange tan, and long hair are what really make somebody confident? Is that what we need to have to be okay, feel good, and even love ourselves? Is it only what's on the outside that counts? Of course not! But it's the message we've been getting since we were old enough to slip into a pair of jeans and ask, "Do these make my butt look big?"

Real self-esteem comes from inside of you. It's about making friends with yourself, listening to yourself, connecting with the inner you, trusting yourself, knowing you are awesome, embracing yourself inside and out, and then, politely but firmly, saying a great big "screw you!" to all the people who make you feel bad about yourself.

The truth is, no amount of money, no "must-haves," and no "it" items can give you self-esteem. It's an inner concept, and it's your birthright. You weren't put here to be a lesser version of yourself or to morph into what other people think you should be. You have everything you need inside you to become the greatest version of you, and that's what you should be doing!

The bottom line, ladies, is that you are too awesome not to be loved by you, and you are missing out on a ton of amazing experiences if you don't start taking control of your life and figuring stuff out based on your inner convictions. Going from poor to stellar self-esteem will totally change your life, your relationships, and how you relate to other people. It won't necessarily make all your problems go away, make you a social butterfly, or make you friends with the "popular" girls, but it will transform the kind of life you lead. Here's how:

If you have high self-esteem:
- You don't need people to validate you.
- You celebrate your friends' successes and good news and are happy for them, without jealousy or feeling competitive.
- You stand up for yourself and resist peer pressure.
- You have a positive outlook on life.
- You try new things and step out of your comfort zone.
- You believe in yourself and have big dreams.
- You like how you look, and you feel comfortable in your skin.

But, if you have low self-esteem:
- You care—a lot—about what people think of you.
- You are easily pressured into doing things you know you shouldn't do, just to "fit in."
- You don't feel "good enough."
- You are an "I can't" gal.
- You make fun of, bully, or pick on other people so that you feel better about yourself.
- You overeat or under eat.
- You hide your body behind baggy clothes.
- You don't step out of your comfort zone or try new things.

The cool thing is, every girl on the planet can have high self-esteem. It's not about being "perfect" or thin or smarter than a rocket scientist; it's about being *you*, right now. Waiting to be different before you can like yourself is the biggest waste of time, ever. Self-esteem only ever comes from within you. It's a decision that *you* get to make about how you feel about you.

Here are some common misconceptions about confidence and self-esteem:

- Only pretty people feel confident.
- If I were more beautiful I would have a perfect life.
- Guys only want to date "hot" girls.
- If I were thinner, my life would be better.
- The only way I'll ever be popular is if I look like the popular girls.

Take it from me, chicas—there is only one version of you, so make it rock! Being an original is way cooler than being like everybody else. I'm pretty sure you already know that, deep down, but I get that it can be hard.

I learned these lessons—and more—in high school. I was dealing with a mentally and verbally abusive mother, and I had a little sister who needed for me to be *her* mother. I changed high schools five times in four years and had struggled with feeling "fat" ever since fifth grade, when I realized that I didn't look like the other girls. I began trying to hide under baggy clothes. I felt really insecure about doing sports activities because I thought my thighs would jiggle, and in my mind, every person on the field was staring at them. Of course, they weren't; I just *felt* like they were, which was enough to keep me on the bench. My mother tried to make me feel as if I was a horrible, terrible person—she told me that every day—and I as much as I didn't believe it, it made me really sad. I was shy, but eventually, I put all my energy into helping my classmates, which, in turn, helped me feel better about myself.

I also stayed focus on my dreams and confided in my dad, who helped me reach my goals and start my business, and he encouraged me to write and dream bigger for myself. I was really lucky to have that focus and to have somebody who made me believe in myself 100 percent. Pretty soon, I became way less shy, got more involved in activities that made me feel good, and got my booty-licious behind off the bench and into the game.

The point is, we all go through pretty rough things, but it doesn't mean that we are doomed to a life of low self-esteem. Whatever has been holding you back, you can overcome it, whether you feel unloved, not good enough, not smart enough, "fat," or not as pretty as your sister. Most important, it's up to you whether you take control of your life and work towards having a healthy relationship with yourself. It's totally up to you to get to know yourself, accept yourself, flaws and all, and treat yourself with dignity and respect. And of course, it's up to you if you want to care about what other people think about you, compare yourself to the airbrushed-within-an-inch-of-their-lives girls in magazines, and try to fit into what you *think* you should be, instead of staying true to yourself. But before I unleash a whole world of tips on you to start being a self esteem queen, let's get a better idea of what self-esteem is … and is *not*.

Healthy vs. Unhealthy Confidence

"I don't want to be perfect, but I do want to be a role model. My mom always tells me that imperfections equal beauty. All of us are imperfect."
—Miley Cyrus, actress, singer

Sometimes, different kinds of behavior can come across as confidence when, in fact, it covers up a lack of it. Don't get confused; here are some types of girls who may appear confident but aren't. Here's how you can figure out for yourself what self-esteem really looks like.

The Stuck-Up Girl: This girl thinks she's better than anyone and considers herself way above everybody else. She may appear strong and self-assured, but she's hiding behind her coldness so she doesn't have to make real connections with people. She's probably making up for super-low self-esteem by putting other people down so she can feel better about herself.

The Mean Girl: Just because she's popular and seems sure of herself doesn't mean she actually is. This girl does everything she can to seem confident, yet on the inside, she usually is super-insecure. She makes fun of other girls, gossips, and puts people down to make herself seem more powerful than she feels inside.

The Tough Girl: Nothing seems to faze her; she has a sarcastic answer for everything and kind of scares the other girls. Just because she seems sure of herself doesn't mean she is, and she's probably acting tough to cover up her pain and insecurities.

When you really do have confidence, you aren't over the top about it, and you don't put people down or think you are above anybody else. You just are who you are, whether you are naturally outgoing, quiet, loud, funny, serious, or whatever. No matter where you are, you feel like yourself, are comfortable, and are able to communicate with the people around you.

Are You Playing a Character?

"Be who you are and say what you feel, because those who matter don't mind, and those who mind don't matter!"
—Dr. Seuss, author

Sometimes, it's easier to be somebody else than it is to be yourself. If you get rejected or dumped when you are playing a role, it's not as hard as being rejected for being *you*. Or maybe you try to be somebody that your boyfriend, friends, or parents want you to be. It's a totally natural way to protect yourself, but if you aren't careful, you'll be using it as something to hide behind, instead of letting your true self shine.

Some popular characters we experiment with in high school are the popular chick, the nerd, the goody-goody, the glamour girl, the bitch, the doormat, the diva, and the I'll-do-whatever-you-want-to-keep-you girl. You might also feel the need to take on certain characteristics to help you feel accepted, such as being bitchy, mean, rude, or taking up drinking or doing drugs, which could lead you down the wrong road pretty quick.

Sometimes your group of gals or the clique you belong to will define who they want you to be, instead of letting you be yourself. Have you ever felt you had to do a certain thing or act a certain way to fit in? That means you are playing a character, and the things you are doing or saying are usually in conflict with who you really are. Here's what you need to know to start being a star in your own life—and leave the role-playing for *Romeo and Juliet*.

Costume: Instead of the dress code imposed by the "directors" (the people in your group), be your own stylist and choose clothes and accessories that reflect you.

Script: Instead of going along with what you think people want you to say, just say what you feel. People respect honesty, and even though your co-stars may disagree with you, don't sweat it. I think it's cool to have your own opinions, and I love it when young women aren't afraid to be true to themselves. But there is a fine line—if you don't like your pal's shoes, there is no need to blurt it out!

Set Design: Shakespeare once wrote: "All the world's a stage …." That's kind of true, so design the stage you're going to star on, rather than being a supporting character on somebody else's stage.

Real Girls, Real Insecurities

"When I lay my head on the pillow at night. I can say I was a decent person today. That's when I feel beautiful. My whole life. I've wanted to feel comfortable in my skin. It's the most liberating thing in the world."
—Drew Barrymore, actress

It's normal to enter your teen years without a whole lot of self-esteem—we all do! You enter teendom as a kid, but by the end of it, you are (hopefully!) a mega-confident, in-control adult. But there are a whole lot of changes that take place in between. If you are struggling with figuring yourself out—who you are, what makes you tick, how you look, what you are or aren't good at, what kind of gal you want to be, how you think you should be, and trying to fit it—join the club! It's totally normal; we all go through the exact same stuff, even if some of us hide it better than others.

If your confidence is MIA (missing in action), don't stress. Most teens feel insecure once in a while. In fact, it is almost impossible to feel confident all the time in your teen years. Here's why:

• You probably haven't figured out who you are yet, so it makes it kind of hard to feel good about yourself when you don't know who that is!
• Sticks and stones *do* break bones—emotional ones, anyway, and that can have serious consequences for a healthy self-esteem.
• You don't feel like you are as pretty, funny, smart, etc., as your friends or the girls on TV.

Think you are the only girl with weird insecurities or less-than-stellar self-confidence? Think again! I surveyed a *ton* of girls to find out the kinds of things they are insecure about, and here are the most common problem areas: Shyness, hygiene issues, big boobs, small boobs, embarrassing parents, not being perfect, high expectations, clothes, mean girls, Hollywood, the media, not being smart enough, hair, weight, grades, goals, boys, dating, sex, changes, pimples, meeting new people, being the new girl, talking to the opposite sex, peer pressure, and pretty much everything else. Crazy, huh? And just so you know, even the girls who seem to have no worries, do have them, too:

*Just because I was **homecoming queen** doesn't mean I didn't have my share of self-esteem issues! I hated my frizzy hair and would spend an hour and a half every day straightening it, and spent hundreds of dollars on products to make my hair look normal. Nobody knew except me, and the*

ironic thing is, I got voted "Best Hair of '05" in my yearbook! I guess I deserved it, because I spent more time and money on it than anyone else!"
—Kierstin, 21

"I was the **valedictorian** for my high school, and I worked really hard to get there. I was proud of myself, but I was so insecure about my weight that I didn't enjoy the experience. I knew I had a lot to say to inspire my class, but it was the hardest thing in the world to get up in front of all my peers. I felt gross, embarrassed, and insecure about my body. I just wished it could end so I could get off stage, and I know I could have done a better job delivering my speech. And the weird thing is, looking back at pictures from that day, I can't believe how good I actually look. I just wish I could have seen it then."
—Donna, 22

"I was considered one of the "**popular**" girls in my high school. I dated a couple of the guys on the football team and was pretty much everything the stereotype portrayed—right down to my eating disorder. Nobody knew how sick I was, how I would throw up after every meal, and how I started taking laxatives to lose even more weight. I was so skinny, and it seemed the more weight I lost, the more other girls would want to be like me. They thought that because I was skinny, I had no worries when, in fact, I was terrified of gaining even an ounce and would weigh myself a couple times a day. Eventually, after graduation, when I reached my lowest weight, ninety-three pounds (I'm five foot four), I looked at myself in the mirror and knew I had to change. I am happy to report that after a couple years of therapy and treatment, I'm on the road to recovery."
—Camille, 21

And celebs, too:

"Have there been times when I've been insecure? Hell, yeah!"
—Ashlee Simpson, singer

Even gals who you think have it all together still have self-esteem issues and insecurities. Which leads me to the question, where did things go wrong? Where, along the line, did we start disliking ourselves? Who told us we weren't good enough? And, who came up with the crazy, narrow-minded standard of beauty and what we should be? We may never know exactly what fostered such a girl-against-girl society, but I dug deep to understand the five most common self-esteem robbers for teen girls:

- The Media. Skinny supermodels, airbrushing, Photoshop, and a permanent "thin is in" attitude made the media girls' numero uno source of insecurity.

- Friends. Lots of you reported wishing you were as pretty, smart, sexy, funny, or as attractive to guys as your BFFs.
- Family. From your mom's perma-diets to your "perfect" older sis, a ton of self-esteem issues start at home, including having an absent dad or abusive parent.
- Guys. It's natural to want to be attractive to the opposite sex, but trying to fit into a dude's idea of "hot" can make you feel like you don't measure up.
- Culture. Different cultures value different things, and living in a society where big boobs are valued over big brains and men still get paid more than women makes lots of you feel "less than" our male counterparts.

Some of the things that affect your self-esteem and self-worth include being called names by your friends or family, being made to feel bad about yourself, having unsupportive people around you, going through your parents' divorce, failing a test, not making the team, and comparing yourself to other girls. But just as the "self-esteem robbers" are numerous, so are the ways to overcome them.

So, here's the truth, gal to gal:

- The teen years are hard. There are always going to be people who you think are prettier, funnier, smarter, sexier, or better in some way than you are. It just doesn't mean they *are*.
- Moods suck. Hormones are swirling, moods are raging, your peaks and valleys are off the charts, and you might feel great about yourself one day and really, really bad the next.
- Bad hair days, fat days, and I-just-want-to-crawl-in-a-hole days happen. Often.
- You won't always make the team, ace the test, get your dream date, or have people love you 100 percent of the time, but you do always have control over how you react in those situations and how you feel about yourself.
- You don't have to be super-thin, super-curvy, super-athletic, super-beautiful or super *anything* to be a confident, happy, successful, rockin' gal! You just have to be you, 100 percent.
- It is nobody's mission in life (except yours) to make you feel great about yourself.
- You do have control over a ton of stuff (remember earlier), including how you feel about and treat yourself.

Now you know the truth and what to expect; it's time to learn how to find the confident gal in you. Hint: *It's not that hard!*

Be a Self-Esteem Queen

"Beauty, to me, is about being comfortable in your own skin. That, or a kick-ass red lipstick."
—Gwyneth Paltrow, actress

Being a self-esteem queen is all about knowing who you are (a goddess), what you are capable of (everything!), and your value (priceless!). Self-esteem queens go for it; they make things happen; they step out of their comfort zones; and they never accept less than what they deserve. They know self-esteem is not something you can catch, touch, find lying around, or receive from somebody else. It is a *feeling*, an inner knowledge that you rock and that you are beautiful, worthy, smart, funny, sexy, wanted, and capable of doing whatever you dream up.

How, you ask, does one become a self-esteem queen, considering all the things we have insecurities about? First of all, give yourself permission *not* to be perfect, and start taking steps to figure out the age-old question: "Who *am* I?"

Away from school, friends, pressure, family, and day-to-day life, "who am I?" is a tough question to answer, but it's super-important to know who you really are on the *inside*. You are a mix of your values, beliefs, morals, thoughts, feelings, talents, interests, ideals, gifts, and life experiences. You are a multi-faceted gem, and it takes time to get to know each part of you. By practicing the following exercises and incorporating them into your daily life, you will feel way more in touch with who you are—and you won't feel so out of whack. Plus, the exercises will help you overcome any roadblocks you face on the road to self-esteem.

Write Your Story

"I write constantly but only in my journals. I have three of them: one for travel, one for home, and one I write in before bed. But the last thing I want is other people reading it."
—Cameron Diaz, actress

A great way to figure out who you are and what makes you tick is by writing in a journal. It can really change your life, and whether you are writing in a beat-up old notebook or a silk-covered, ribbon-tied masterpiece, it'll help you discover the inner you. It's amazing what happens when you collect your thoughts, feelings, ideas, hopes, fears, dreams, and discoveries in one place, organize them, and take a look at your life in its pages. Maybe you'll figure out how you *really* feel about your parents' split and the effect it's *actually* having on your life, or why you and your mom fight so much.

MySpace blogs and Facebook posts are great, but can you ever really be completely real, honest, and authentic when you know hundreds of people are going to be reading it? I know I never could! There was always that voice in the back of my head, wondering what people would think. That's the cool thing about having a journal—you can keep it hidden under your bed (or wherever!), and you can reveal the inner you, be honest about your problems, and express your innermost feelings, because you are the only one who is gonna read it! No pretending, faking, or hiding the real you.

Try the following journal exercises to start today:

- Gratitude: What are you most grateful for? It's easy to lose sight of the great things about your life when there is so much drama happening all around you, so by writing down the top five things you are grateful for each day, you'll be focused on what's great about your life instead of everything that's wrong with it.
- Write yourself a letter: This is a really cool thing to do. Sit down, and write yourself a letter from you—to *you*! Explain how you feel about you, what you love, what you are confused about, what you want to change, what you want help with, and who you want to become. You could also

try writing a letter to the child version of you (inner child, anyone?), or you could write as if you are the adult you writing to the present-day you and telling her everything she needs to know.

- Q & A: I like to do this one because it makes me rely on me and not on outside sources to solve problems. Don't get me wrong; those outside sources can be really important, but it's really interesting to answer my own questions and solve my own problems, too. Write down a question about something that's been confusing you, close your eyes and take a couple deep breaths, and then find the answer *inside* you. Keep going until all your questions are answered—at least for now!

If you are anything like me, you'll be totally pumped about this, go out, buy a notebook, bling it out, and write in it for three nights, before it eventually turns into an ornament on your bedside table instead of a really great get-to-know-yourself manual! No worries; here are some tips to get you started—and motivated to keep going:

- Make it personal: You don't have to spend a ton of money on a fancy journal, you can make your own. Go to your local craft store, and pick up a cheap notebook, some pretty papers, fabrics, paints, glue, glitter, ribbon, fake flowers, stickers, or beads, and unleash your inner designer!
- Commit to yourself to write in it every day—for a month: It might seem like a big commitment, but science shows us that it takes thirty days for our brains to make a new habit stick. It'll be even better if you do it around the same time every day, too, to really get in the habit. Making a ritual out of it makes it more fun and will make you more likely to keep it up. For example, why don't you make yourself a cup of herbal tea (or, if that's not your thing, a beverage of your choice), slip into your p.j.'s, get into bed, and write for five or ten minutes? Did I mention the square of chocolate you eat when you are finished? Now that's a ritual worth sticking to!
- Be creative: You don't have to just *write*. How about expressing yourself through photos, making collages, drawing, painting, or sketching your feelings, emotions, or scenes from you day? Or, how about including notes from friends, song lyrics, your favorite poems, pictures of your mentors and role models, or even swatches of fabric from old clothes that have important memories for you?

Once your month is up, read over your journal and see if you notice any patterns or word associations. Did "love" and "music" show up in more than one sentence together? Maybe the inner you is trying to tell you something! Try signing up for music lessons or songwriting classes. Pay attention to your innermost wants, needs, ideas, and feelings, and be an "actionista"—which means taking action to let the inner you shine.

Get a New Soundtrack

Whether or not you know it, you have an inner soundtrack or mantra. Dictionary.com describes "mantra" as "A commonly repeated word or phrase; a sacred verbal formula repeated in prayer, meditation, or incantation, such as an invocation of a god, a magic spell, or a syllable or portion of scripture containing mystical potentialities." So basically, the things you say over and over in your head have way more power than you might think! That's why it's important to make the things you repeat to yourself, over and over again, positive rather than negative! Unfortunately, what you're saying over and over in your head might sound something like this:

- I'm not good enough.
- I'll never be able to run fast enough to make the team.
- I'm not pretty enough for him to notice me.
- I'm not as smart as my sister.
- I'll never amount to anything.
- I'm way too fat (thin/tall/short).

Ouch! Our mantras can kind of hurt! No wonder you don't like yourself sometimes! If you recognize your mantra here, ask yourself how that's been working for you so far. Probably not great, right?

Has it held you back from trying out for a team or sport you love? Were you a no-show at an audition? Did you boycott the babe you've been crushing on? What you repeat over and over to yourself becomes the truth. If you tell me you aren't good enough to make the team, I believe you. Why? It's not because I think you aren't good enough; I just believe that it's true because *you* believe it's true. You are only as good as you think you are. If you don't think you can do something, you can't. If you do, you can. It's as simple as that.

With that said, I want you to close your eyes and think about your inner soundtrack. What kind of things do you repeat over and over again in your head? Hopefully, some are positive, but focus for a sec on the negative ones. Get a pen and paper and write them down, exactly how you repeat them to yourself, just like the ones above. Once you have them written down, I want you to rip and tear up that paper into tiny shreds and throw it out the window and watch it blow away, toss it in the fireplace, or throw it in the trash. Now, it is gone, and it's time to find a new playlist!

Upgrade!

If you are going to repeat things over and over in your head, make them positive, inspiring words of encouragement.

Let's take a cue from Ugly Betty herself. Remember in the first episode when she repeats to herself, "I am a smart, successful business woman"? You need to do that, too! Next time you tell yourself that you aren't good enough, stop, and re-program yourself with "I am strong, smart, and capable of doing whatever I set my mind to."

The cool thing is, people pay thousands of dollars for success coaches who tell them stuff like that. Now, you have one built right in!

My new mantra is:_____

_____

After you become more in touch with who you are, start doing things to make that girl come alive and share her with the world. The more you take control of your life and take action, instead of just sitting back and letting other people make decisions for you, the more you will shine.

Meditate

You probably think that meditation is about people sitting crossed-legged and chanting, but it's actually way easier than that. It's a great way to manage your stress and connect to your inner gal. Here's all you need to do:

Find a quiet place where you can sit or lie down comfortably, without being disturbed, and close your eyes. Start focusing on your breathing, and feel your body relax. From there, you can do all kinds of things. Here are some ideas:

- Explore the inner you: Connect to yourself, who you are, what you love, what makes you tick, and who you want to become. Ask yourself those questions, and take the first answers that pop into your head.
- Get in touch with your body: Start from your baby toe up to the top of your head. Really *feel* your body. Ask it what it needs more of or less of, and you can even tell it or ask it whatever you want.
- Connect with your higher self or inner guide. It could be a person or just a feeling. Explore it!
- Explore your inner soundtrack: Repeat your positive mantras over and over again in your mind.

"My dad had a really stressful job, and when he retired, he started getting into tons of Eastern stuff, like yoga and meditation. He taught me one [meditation] that I totally fell in love with, where you picture a really bright, violet flame inside you, and you focus on that while you keep breathing really deep. It made me so much more spiritual, and I couldn't believe how relaxed I felt. It only takes, like, ten minutes a day, but it makes a huge difference."
—Lynette, 17

See? It's not that hard to start getting a better idea of what makes you tick. And you might be surprised by how much cooler you are than you may have thought! And now that you are on a confidence-gaining roll, here's more stuff you can do to go out there and get it, because it won't just show up at your door one day; you have find it and feel it *inside*.

"Why should I care what other people think of me? I am who I am. And who I wanna be."
—Avril Lavigne, singer

Be an Actionista

You may have heard the saying that "life rewards action." I *totally* believe that and have proved it to myself, time and time again. If you take action and go after something, you are more likely to find it than if you just sit at home and wait for it to happen. Here are some ways you can take action and put in the necessary work to *earn* your confidence badge.

- Do more of the stuff that makes you feel good about yourself and less of the stuff that makes you feel bad about yourself. That means getting up and going for a jog or taking a dance class, instead of reading tabloids.
- Speak up. If your family is making you feel bad by being sarcastic or joking about stuff that makes you insecure, let them know, and ask them to stop. They might not know that their "joking" hurts your feelings.
- Encourage yourself. Tell yourself the same stuff you'd tell your friends to make them feel good, and encourage yourself the same way you would encourage them when it comes to taking risks and going after your dreams.
- Surround yourself with people who have interests, hobbies, goals, dreams, values, ideas, and morals similar to yours. You'll feel way more "at home" with them—and with yourself.
- Look for validation inside as well as outside. There is nothing like an "atta girl" from somebody you look up to and admire to boost your self-esteem, so surround yourself with great role models who are willing to mentor you.
- Try new things. From ballet to escargot, try as many new things as possible. It will expand your horizons and give you more life experience to draw from. Plus, you'll feel proud of yourself for taking risks.
- Help others. Volunteer in your community, or help a fellow gal pick up the contents of her binder that splattered all over the hallway. Helping other people makes you feel *great*!
- Sign up for a singing (or acting or dance) class to learn new ways to express yourself and connect with your body.
- Get together with guys and gals who are into the same stuff as you. If you love comics, horror movies, coin collecting, or whatever, find a group of peeps who love it, too! You'll feel way more confident if you are around people who "get" you and your interests.

- Join your school's debate team, drama club, or public- speaking class to gain confidence in speaking to others.
- Take quiet walks—no iPods allowed. Quiet time by yourself helps you connect with the inner you and figure stuff out.
- Worried about the way you talk or read? Practice! If you have a physical feature that you are super-uncomfortable about, find ways to play up other parts of you that you love, or cleverly disguise the "offending" part with makeup or clothing. If you hate the sound of your own voice (like I did; ironic, don't you think?), practice talking and reading out loud so you get confident with it. If it's a bigger issue than just lacking confidence, get speech therapy, get help reading, or talk to a professional. And remember, your peers are usually way more concerned about their own issues than yours.
- Surround yourself with stuff that reflects *you*! If you feel comfortable in your surroundings and feel that you are reflected in your own space, it'll help you to embrace who you are. If you are at your home, decorate your room in your favorite color or theme, and choose clothes that represent you. At school, stick stuff in your locker that inspires and motivates you to achieve your goals, and wear clothes that show your personality.
- Distance yourself from the people who make you feel worse about yourself. You have just as much right to share your opinion as anybody else, and if the people around you make you feel like you don't matter, ditch them for people who do. (See lesson 2 for tips on spotting toxic friends and finding new ones.)
- Practice! If there is a guy/gal in your class you want to get to know better, practice having the conversation you want to have with him or her in your head so you get confident with what you want to say. Try to work out different kinds of situations, in case it doesn't go as planned.
- Crank up your stereo and dance around your room, singing at the top of your lungs. It will rev you up and put you in a great, confident frame of mind.
- Name one thing that you love about yourself every day, while standing in front of the mirror. "I love how I always smell so good" or "I love how funny I am" are great ways to start.
- Press the mental "reject" button if anybody calls you a name, says something mean, or tries to label you. It's all about *them* and so not a reflection on you. Or, you could picture yourself in a giant

bubble that only lets good things in and reflects the negative stuff back to whoever sent it.

- Stick up for yourself or your friends. It takes a ton of courage; don't worry if you can't do it right away. Start by *thinking about* how you would stick up for yourself, and then, when you are ready, actually do it. You will feel really great afterward.

If you are still struggling with feeling confident, there is one last resort. You can always **fake it 'til you make it**!

Fake It 'til You Make It!

"Some people say that I have an attitude. Maybe I do. But I think that you have to. You have to believe in yourself when no one else does—that makes you a winner right there."
—Venus Williams, champion tennis player

You know that old saying, practice makes perfect? It's true, and it totally applies to confidence, too. Nobody wakes up one day and walks out the house like a superstar. It takes time, effort, and work. But there are some ways to speed it along. Curious? Keep reading!

Act Confident

You don't have to actually feel confident to act confident. And the cool thing is, if you do act confident, you will start to feel confident, too. It's like magic or science or something. Here's how:

- Stand up straight and hold your head high. You will come across like a self-esteem queen. Remind yourself of standing this way throughout the day, and keep it up. Pretty soon, it will come naturally.
- Laugh at yourself. Yup, sometimes when we take ourselves too seriously, we get way too caught up in trying to be perfect. If you do something super–cringe-worthy, blow it off. Stuff like that happens to everybody. You'll look really confident if you can take yourself less seriously.
- When I was faced with situations that I felt less confident about, I'd always picture the worst case scenario (WCS) and freak myself out even more—until I turned it all around. I pictured the *best* case scenario. I went over it in my head and saw it ending up exactly how I wanted it to. I still do it all the time, and it puts me in the right frame of mind to feel confident in the situation.

- Do it anyway! Confident people take risks. I was scared to write this book, start my business, and speak at high schools. I felt a mega-lack of confidence when I walked out in front of my first audience. But I did it anyway, and I felt so amazing afterward! Sure, my knees were knocking, but I went on autopilot, words came out, and I got applause when I was finished. Scary stuff gets easier each time you do it, so do it anyway!
- Make eye contact when you talk to people. Experts say about 75 percent of eye contact during a conversation shows that you are confident and that you are paying attention.
- Smile: A megawatt smile lights up a room and makes you seem super-inviting, open, cool, and fun to be around.
- Insecure about the negative things people say about you? Yup, that sucks. But instead of showing people that their negative opinions bother you, act like it's no biggie. If they see you are strong and don't give a shiz about what they say, they'll soon move on, leaving you to keep getting more and more confident. Voila!
- Beyoncé, from the musical group Destiny's Child, has an alter ego named Sasha when she is on stage. Sasha is the more confident, sexy version of Beyoncé. I thought that was a good idea, and when I speak at high schools, or when I'm confronted with a super-big audience, I have a more confident alter ego, too. Why don't you make one up for yourself? She's the outgoing, confident, bubbly version of you that is there whenever you need her!

Dress Confident

It's not fair, but the world—and your peers—judge you on how you dress and present yourself. The clothes you choose in the morning affect how people treat you all day long. It doesn't mean you should or shouldn't dress a certain way, or that one way is better than the other. But being aware of what you say to the world will help you navigate your way through it and end up with what you want.

Figure out what you want to say to the world *before* you get dressed in the morning. If you want to say "I'm confident and smart; take me seriously!" then you'll have to dress in a way that conveys that, so skip the baby T's and fishnets! Here are a couple of tips to make sure your clothes are working for ya:

- Have a couple pieces of clothes that reflect different moods. If you want to feel full of energy, grab the yellow T, or if you want to feel sophisticated and serious, opt for the navy or black dress with dark leggings and a cute cardigan.

- Take an extra five minutes and pull yourself together. No, not your mood, but that helps, too; I mean your outfit. I can't say enough for belts, cute earrings, some fun pieces of jewelry, and a matching bag. You'll look super-chic and pulled together, no matter what your style is, and feel more confident, too.
- Ever wear something to fit in with a certain group, but it was so uncomfortable that you ended up feeling *less* cool instead? Wear stuff that makes you feel good and that you don't have to worry about. Who can feel comfortable, wondering if her thong is poking out the back of her jeans each time she bends over? Not me! And remember, comfortable doesn't mean frumpy. Pick a favorite part of your body, and play that up instead of following crazy trends.
- Wear stuff that *you* love, not your friends, or your mom, or what you see in the magazines. If you love it, you'll feel comfortable in it, which will make you feel more confident.

"Don't let anyone tell you that you have to be a certain way. Be unique. Be what you feel."

—Melissa Etheridge, singer-songwriter

Bodacious Body-Lovin Gal

"It's not about weight—it's about caring for yourself on a daily basis."
—Oprah Winfrey

"I didn't always love my body. You have to learn to be okay with yourself. This is the body you are stuck with."

—Hayden Panettiere, actress

I don't believe I have ever met one who didn't have some sort of body-image blahs, no matter how confident, "perfect," or pretty she seemed. And you know all those celebs we love so much? They have body issues, too! Every girl is self-conscious about something to do with her body, especially in her teen years. Things are growing, moving, changing, and becoming utterly unfamiliar from what they were just a few short years ago. Combine that with a society that's pretty much obsessed with crazy-thin, "perfect" girls, and we are left with a pretty messed up idea of how we should feel about our bodies, which in turn affects our self-esteem. Here are some stats on body image from the Dove Campaign for Real Beauty.

- Ninety-two percent of teen girls would like to change something about the way they look, with body weight ranking the highest.

- Seventy-five percent of teenage girls felt "depressed, guilty, and shameful" after spending just three minutes leafing through a fashion magazine.

- Seventy percent of girls aged fifteen to seventeen avoid normal daily activities, such as attending school, going to the doctor, or even giving their opinion, "due to feeling badly about [their] looks."

- Nearly twenty-five percent would consider undergoing plastic surgery.

- Only two percent of women describe themselves as "beautiful."

Why do we feel so bad about our bods as a society of young women, in general? It's obvious that the media wreaks the most havoc on how we feel about our bodies. Here's a Top Five list of what you need to know about it.

1. There are not two kinds of people, the models and the people who want to look like the models. The models are cartoon versions of themselves; even they don't look like the way we see them portrayed. We are being manipulated as much as the photographs are.

2. Ever heard of "vanity sizing"? Me, either, until I did a little research. Clothing stores and designers get to make up their own sizes, and usually, they make them a little smaller than the actual size to get you to think you are a size 2 (when you might be a 4 or a 6), so that you will buy their clothes!

3. If somebody could bottle Photoshop and other digital-image enhancers so that they worked on real people instead of photographs, they would be best sellers! Unfortunately, every picture you see in magazines or on billboards has been enhanced or touched up, and as you know, real girls like you and me don't have a personal retoucher to follow us around!

4. Most of the ladies in the pages of the mags sat for hours as someone worked on their makeup, hair, tan, body shimmering, back-fat taping, and tons of other stuff so they would look "perfect." How many of us have our very own beauty teams?

5. Advertisers are sneaky and have billions of dollars at their disposal. They use those billions to target you, and to make you feel bad about yourself so you will buy their wonder product to fix it; they bombard you everywhere you look. Did you know they try to place their ads close to schools, malls, and other places teens go? That's because teen gals are huge business for them.

"I disappoint people who meet me in person because I don't look like me."
—Tyra Banks, model

"Even I don't wake up looking like me."
—Cindy Crawford, model

"It's all make-believe, isn't it?
—Marilyn Monroe, 1950s film star

Crazy, right? Here's what you need to do to be media smart:

- **Think** about what you are seeing and hearing; don't just accept it as reality.

- **Ask** yourself how those ads/mags/TV shows make you feel. Do you really feel bad about yourself, or do you feel bad that they try so hard to make girls like you think there is stuff wrong with them that only certain products can "fix"?

- **Write** to your local TV stations, magazines, and companies targeting youth and let them know how you and your friends feel when you see those ads. Bonus points if you boycott them until they change their strategies!

- **Know** that what you see is totally fake, made up and strategically enhanced.

And while you are at it, why not start doing stuff every day to connect with your body, learn to be okay with it, and maybe even start to like it a little?

Dear Bod...

You are totally used to talking *about* your body, but what would you say if you were talking *to* it instead? I can tell you a million tips, go over everything that's worked for me or other girls, and go on and on for days about the media, Photoshop, and how everything we see is just an illusion anyway. But it won't necessarily make a difference to *you*. Here's why: It has to be your idea to start to love your body; nobody can make you change the way you see yourself but you. So, here's what I want you to do:

1. Get a pen and paper, and find somewhere cozy to sit where you can write.

2. Play your favorite music, dim the lights, light candles, burn some incense—whatever makes you feel relaxed. (You can even take a bath first, slather on some lavender lotion, and totally get chilled out that way!)

3. Start the letter with "Dear Body …" and complete it from there. Tell your body how you feel about it, what you like about it, what you don't like about it, what you want to change, what you are proud of, what you are sorry for, what you are angry about, etc. Let it all out, and don't hold back. Remember, nobody is going to read it but you, unless you want them to. (If you are really worried about somebody finding your letter, rip it up, burn it, or shred it after you're finished.)

To help you get started, I'll share my letter to my body:

Dear Body,

We have been through a lot together. I guess, first of all, I'd like to thank you for everything. We've had our ups and downs for sure. Sometimes I think you are too big, or there is too much of you to love. Sometimes I get annoyed, having to remove all the hair, and I guess it would be cool if you wouldn't jiggle so much! But I do love and respect you, and I try to do everything I can to keep you safe. I'm sorry about your left arm and all it pain it feels. I wish it were stronger and healthier, but I'm really nervous about the surgery. Apart from that, I want to thank you for being healthy and strong. You have taken me so many places and are just as good as those "thin" bods we see on TV all the time. In fact, I think you are cuter! Thank you for being with me on stages across the country—and not shaking too much! I think you are really beautiful, flaws and all, and I will learn to accept you fully, more and more every day, because I am grateful to you for being the vehicle in which I live my life. I know

I am more than you, and one day we will part, but for now, I am going to enjoy our relationship. And I pledge to do one nice thing for you every day, and give you one nice compliment each morning before we start our day together.
xoxo
Kate

Your turn! And remember, going from no or low confidence about your body to having a ton if confidence won't happen overnight. It's just a matter of doing small things, every day, to help you feel better about yourself. And give yourself a break, already!

Body-Loving Tips

• Stop "fat" talk. That means body-bashing with your pals, telling your friends how "ugly" you feel that day, or telling yourself that you are "disgusting," "too fat," or anything else that's cruel! For the next week, treat your body like your friend. Only say stuff to it (or about it) that you would say to your BFF. Having trouble? Wear an elastic on your wrist, and snap it each time you say something snarky about yourself. You'll learn pretty quickly to be positive!

• Avoid stuff that makes you feel bad. Remember the study above that said 75 percent of teen girls feel bad about themselves after reading a fashion mag? If you are one of them, don't look through one for a month. Or, if you feel bad watching overly glamorized TV shows, switch them off, and go for a walk or do something else that makes you feel good. Spend some time now thinking about what your "good body image" and "bad body image" triggers are. For me, sitting down in front of the TV, munching on chips, makes me feel less than great about myself. On the other hand, I feel great about my body when I'm doing Pilates or yoga—especially when it's all done! I also feel great hanging out with people who love and accept me exactly how I am. What can you think of to replace your bad triggers?

• Create a "Good Body Image" scrapbook, filled with pics of

people you really admire for their inner beauty as much as their outer beauty. Who seems super-confident in her own skin? Get a variety of women with all kinds of different body shapes, sizes, and colors. I'd have pics of America Ferrera, Queen Latifah, Catherine Zeta-Jones, Oprah, etc. Also, include your favorite pics of yourself, song lyrics or poems that inspire you ("Phenomenal Woman" by Maya Angelou is a must!), and whatever else really makes you feel great.

- For one week, get a journal, and write in it one thing you think is beautiful about your body. Whether it's your hands, feet, earlobes, belly button, eyelashes, fingernails, or the tip of your nose, it doesn't matter. Just pick something every day that you love, and do something special to play it up. For instance, if you are particularly digging your ears, put your hair back and wear some pretty earrings.

- Dance! Crank the tunes and dance around like crazy. I don't know what it is about this, but you will be totally digging you body moving around, totally uninhibited. It's like a bonding experience for you and your bod.

- Work out. There's more on this coming up, but I'm mentioning it here because it is super-important to take care of your body from the inside out. Plus, exercising releases endorphins, which make you feel really good!

- Treat your body! Bubble baths, yummy lotions, and at-home spa treatments help you connect with your body, and the better you make it feel, the more you are going to love it!

- Help your friends feel better about their bodies by complimenting them or by stopping them when they are in the middle of a body-bashing rant and focusing their attention on the positive things about their body.

- Remember that who you are is way more important than the number on your scales, or how tall, short, big, small, or whatever you are!

"The real secret to total gorgeousness is to believe in yourself, have self-confidence, and try to be secure in your decisions and thoughts."
—Kirsten Dunst, actress

Gal to Gal

"I know it is hard, but just be yourself, 100 percent. It gets way easier, and you'll have a way better idea about who you are, which helps when it comes to making the right decisions for you."
—Rhonda, 19

"Try to treat yourself like you treat other people. It's kind of like the reverse of the Golden Rule. My mom always told me that, and it's helped me be way nicer to myself!"
—Grace, 14

"No matter what your body looks like, love it and be grateful for it."
—Caroline, 17

"Find a style that works for you, and don't be scared to try new things. The bottom line is, hair grows back, piercings heal, and you can always buy new clothes!"
—Alicia, 16

Hey, it's okay to:
- Cry, be upset, and be moody. You're a teen girl; it'd be weird if you didn't act that way.
- Draw horns and devil tails on the girls in the magazines. Just kidding!
- Have no clue right now about who you want to be "when you grow up." You'll figure it out before you get there, I promise!
- Actually like your body, flaws and all.
- Be the only one not body-bashing in the bathroom at school with your pals. You deserve better!
- Wear stuff that makes you feel great, whether it's "in" or not.
- Not want to be anything less than a size 14. Big is beautiful, too!

- Stay tuned—the next lesson is all about friends, so don't skip it if you want to learn a whole bunch of tips on making great friends, being a great friend, and riding (and surviving!) the friend-o-coaster!

Lesson 2:
Friendly Gal 101

Friends rock! I'm pretty sure that no matter who you are, where you are from, or what kind of music you are into, you can agree with me on that! But, with that said, friends can be super-complicated too, right? It's hard to figure out who your real friends are, who is a "toxic" friend, and how to balance friends with the rest of your life. And what about dealing with the Queens of Mean, standing up for yourself, and figuring out how to be a good friend yourself? Girl friendships are a tricky thing, but if you figure it all out, the rewards are pretty phenomenal!

"Friendship with oneself is all-important because without it, one cannot be friends with anyone else in the world."
—Eleanor Roosevelt, former First Lady of the U.S., civil rights advocate

Life is full of important decisions; so are friendships. You need to decide what kind of friend you want to be (good, great, not so great), what kinds of friends you want to have, how you will choose your friends (popularity and social standing or compatibility and integrity?), and how centered you are going to become on them. The truth is, those are pretty much the only things you control when it comes to friendships, along with how you will react when a friendship goes bad. Not only that, but these are decisions you are going to have to make every day for the rest of your life. Friendships can be tricky, especially for us gals, and especially in this day and age. We have to deal with mean girls, toxic or fair-weather "friends," and some major hurtful stuff, like cyber bullying and gossip. The good news, it will get easier as you get older (and after I give you a ton of tips, strategies, and advice to make your friendships great!). But before we get into it, here's another "IQ" quiz. Answer the following questions with a 1, 2, or 3.

What's Your Friendly Gal IQ?

1 = No way; 2 = Sorta, sometimes; 3 = Sure do!

1) My friends make me feel good about myself.	1	2	3
2) I have a good balance of friends, school, and family.	1	2	3
3) My friends are loyal, caring, and supportive.	1	2	3
4) I feel confident enough to resist peer pressure.	1	2	3
5) I know I don't have to compromise myself to fit in.	1	2	3
6) I don't put my friends down to feel good about myself.	1	2	3
7) I am considered a good friend.	1	2	3
8) I do what I can to be there for my friends.	1	2	3
9) I know my value as a friend.	1	2	3
10) My friends appreciate me.	1	2	3

Now add up the numbers and find your Friendly Gal IQ. **Total:** _____

10-15: Maybe you have a ton of toxic "friends," are between friends right now, don't know what to look for in good, awesome gal (or guy) pals, and are probably not getting a whole lot out of the relationships you have. But fear not, my friend; it doesn't have to be like this forever. You just need to get clear on what you really want and get to know yourself a little better, and you'll be on track in no time.

16-22: Are friends great or are friends great? I'm pretty sure you'd agree with me, and it looks like you have tons of friend stuff figured out but are probably struggling with some of the inevitable ups and downs of the friend-o-coaster. But with a few more bits and pieces of advice, you'll be on your way to stellar friendships in no time, or at least dealing with a whole lot less drama.

23-30: Looks like your Friendly Gal IQ is right where it should be, and you are probably enjoying some pretty fulfilling relationships, even if once in a while you feel like you are on an episode of some teen-angst–filled TV drama. But even though you can't control your friends and their antics, you totally control you and how you react, no matter what.

Whether your score is hovering around a 10 or is almost off the charts, this chapter is going to do for your friendships what a total home makeover would do for your house! In "Finding, Being, and Making Friends," you'll learn just that, and learn the basic keys to friend success. In "Surviving the Friend-O-Coaster," you'll learn all about surviving the ups and downs of friendship by becoming you-centered (in a good way), figure out how to fix friendships, and how to cope when they fall apart. Then, you'll learn how to deal with toxic friends and mean girls in—you guessed it—"Toxic Friends and Mean Girls."

Finding, Making, and Being Friends

"I used to think my now BFF was stuck up because she was a cheerleader. but we were lab partners together in eighth grade. and now we are so close. I learned that I shouldn't judge somebody before I know [her]."
—Carmen, 17

"Julie and I have been friends since we sat together in first grade. At first. we only had our first name in common. but then we realized. as we grew up. we were so similar. We both want to be in the fashion world. and both of us grew up without a dad. We've been supporting each other ever since!"
—Julie, 16

"I have a group of best friends. It's kind of like in The Sisterhood of the Traveling Pants. except we have a bracelet we pass around. not a pair of jeans!"
—Rebecca, 14

The cool thing about friends is that the right ones usually find each other, like there is some kind of invisible magnetic pull. The most important thing you need to remember when it comes to making, being, or keeping friends is to be yourself. If you dress the way you like, listen to the music that rocks your socks, do the stuff that you love, and be your own gal, you will attract people to you who have similar interests, hobbies, and ideas. These are the chicas you want to be friends with! It's always up to you who you hang around with, what kind of people you are going to surround yourself with, and what kind of gal you are going to be. But what makes a good friend, anyway?

"A good friend is somebody who forgives you."
—Amanda, 16

"I think a good friend is somebody who doesn't judge you. accepts you for who you are. and supports your dreams."
—Steph, 17

"I knew that Shelby was my best friend when I was sick in the hospital. Not only was she there every single day after school, but she got my entire grade to sign a huge get-well card for me, and she collected money to buy me a huge stuffed bear! That was seven years ago, and we are still soul sisters! I'd do anything for her, and she proved she'd do anything for me."
—Diane, 21

"Support, loyalty, love, kindness, and acceptance. That's what I look for in all my friends"
—Jill, 15

As you can see, being a good friend means different things to different people, but here are what most gals consider the most important qualities in a friend:

Good friends:
- Are supportive through good times and bad.
- Are loyal, trustworthy secret-keepers.
- Listen to you—really listen.
- Know you, your flaws, and love you like a sister anyway.
- Laugh and cry with you.
- Celebrate your achievements like they would their own.
- Don't steal your boyfriend.
- Can be totally goofy with you and understand you like nobody else.
- Bring over a pint of ice cream, chick flicks, and magazines if you are heartbroken.

Good friends—really, really good friends—are hard to find, but once you do, they will be like sisters (or brothers) to you, so it's really worth investing in your friendships and taking the time to find friends who are right for you. The best friendships aren't based on popularity or social status; they're formed on a common understanding and connection that goes beyond what's on the outside. And remember, whether you are friends with all girls, all guys, or a combo, this still applies, but for the sake of avoiding he/she or she/he, I am just gonna focus mostly on girl friendships here.

Your Guide to Making Friends

For some people, making friends comes as naturally as Pamela Anderson's ta-tas, while others have more friends than they know what to do with. If you are friendless because you are the new gal, if your old pals had a hissy fit and ditched you (*what were they thinking?*), if you discovered your friends had a toxic nature and you bailed, or if you are just trying to find new friends that fit the new you, it's important to take a chill pill and not rush into anything. The worst thing a gal can do is leap into the first group that expresses an interest, just to avoid the uncomfortable "where am I gonna sit at lunch?" feeling. Take your time, get to know people, and *choose* who you are going to associate with. For those of you who need a little help finding friends, here are some tips:

- Be yourself. If you are acting a part (remember the lesson on self-esteem?), then you will most likely attract people who are like the part you are playing, which is not great for either one of you. Being fake to fit in is doing a major disservice to you and robbing you of opportunities to make real friends. Be true to yourself, and you will attract people who have similar values, goals, and ideas, which are important building blocks for a great relationship.
- Get out there (figuratively and literally). Do you wish you had more or better friends? Then don't miss out on friend-making opportunities; put yourself out there and make some connections. Join a school club you are interested in, volunteer for a cause you believe in, join a youth group, or sign up for a team. You will meet people with the same interests as you and are practically guaranteed to have something in common. Take action and make it happen.
- Be friendly. If you are nice to people, are honest, treat people with respect, smile, laugh, seem comfortable with yourself, and help people out, people are going to be drawn to you, naturally.
- Take initiative. It takes guts, especially if you are shy, but if you see a cool girl who seems like she's as lost as you, strike up a convo and see if she wants to chill at lunch. Hint: She probably will be so relieved, she won't say no!
- Keep an open mind: Don't write people off based on your initial judgment. So what if they look different, are into a different kind of music, or come from a different background? Give them a chance, and get to know them. You never know what you might have in common, even if it's not totally obvious right away. Just because she looks a little different from you doesn't mean she's not totally awesome.

"My best friend. Kath. isn't the type of girl I'm usually friends with. [When I first met her. she] wore baggy pants and didn't wear makeup or do her hair. I'm the opposite—a total girly-girl. I love makeup and getting dressed up. We were in the same art class. and one day we paired up for a class project. We discovered we had a bunch of cool stuff in common. We were both army brats and had moved around a lot. and we both had family members in Iraq. We totally bonded. and four years later. we are still best friends. I'm really glad I got to know her. instead of just thinking we were too different."
—Georgette, 19

Strengthening the Bonds of Sisterhood:
Becoming Better Friends

No matter where your rank in the social food chain that is high school, if you are a good friend, you are practically guaranteed to end up with good friends. By mastering the following five tips, you will enjoy healthier, more supportive friendships.

1. **Communicate!** I know you probably spend hours chatting, Facebooking, and IM'ing, but by "communicate," I mean *really* communicate. Like, tell each other how you feel about difficult topics. For instance, does it hurt your feelings that she blows off her plans with you for her boyfriend? Having the guts to be honest with each other about big-deal things will only make the relationship stronger and get you through difficult times. Plus, having somebody you can talk to about important things in your life is a great way to stay stress-free and figure stuff out.

2. **Get to know each other:** I mean *really* get to know each other. Sharing secrets and personal stuff will make you a lot closer. Go to the library, and get one of those books that asks all the crazy questions, like *The Book of Questions* or *If (Questions for the Game of Life)*, and find out a ton about each other, silly and serious, like what kind of insect you would permanently remove from the earth, or the one thing you would change

about your childhood and why.

3. **Make a pact:** Not a pact to be BFFs but a pact to be honest with each other about difficult stuff, from bad haircuts to bad boyfriends. It can be hard to see stuff clearly when you are in the middle of a bad relationship, getting into the wrong crowd, or making unhealthy decisions. Having somebody to be the voice of wisdom in those situations might help you see what's going on a little better.

4. **Have gal dates:** Sounds weird, but make time in your hectic schedules for each other. It's especially important as you get older—and definitely when you start dating and spend most of your time with your guy. Penciling in your pals for a lunch date will keep the relationship going strong.

5. **Support, encourage and celebrate each other:** The great thing about friends is that you can celebrate in their successes and achievements as much as your own, and have a ton more fun! Be there for each other, and do fun, spontaneous things to encourage and celebrate each other.

"My mom always tells me to celebrate everyone's uniqueness. I like the way that sounds!"

—Hilary Duff, actress, recording artist

The Good Friend Tune-Up

A car needs a tune-up every now and again to keep it running smoothly, and your friendships are no different. If you want good friends, you have to *be* a good friend. Here are some questions to ask yourself to make sure you are being a good friend:

- Do I talk about myself, my life, my family, and my goals more than I ask my friends about theirs?
- Do I have good self-esteem, or do I put down people or make fun of them to make myself feel better?
- Do I feel jealous or in competition with any of my friends, or am I supporting them, encouraging them, and celebrating in their success?
- Do I give my friends the space they need, or am I the girl version of Velcro?

By making some minor adjustments based on your honest answers, such as being more thoughtful, asking about your friends, doing stuff that makes you feel better about yourself, working on being sisters instead of rivals, and having more "you time" and giving your friends theirs, you'll keep your friendships running smoothly.

"One of the best ways for me and my friends to not drive each other crazy is to give each other our space. If we do too much together, we start to get on each other's nerves. Plus, it's super-important to have other focuses outside of our friends so we can really grow and develop our own interests. I feel that if it's meant to be, then it's meant to be, you know?"

—Jessica, 17

Surviving the Friend-O-Coaster

Friendships are full of ups and downs—just like a roller coaster. The ups are awesome and filled with celebrations, parties, hanging out together, and feeling supported and accepted. The downs, however, include dealing with popularity, mean girls, gossip, back-stabbing, and competition, which are, unfortunately, all pretty common things in high school.

But just because your friendships can be all over the place doesn't mean you have to be. Here are some roller-coaster guidelines!

Go from Friend-Centered to You-Centered

Being self-centered is usually not a good thing, but being "you-centered" is a whole other story. It means being centered, or focused, on your goals, dreams, morals, and values, all things you have control over. If your friends are the center of your universe, which (let's face it) is super-common, you are making them responsible for your happiness, success, and confidence. Still don't think it's a big deal? No matter how much you love your friends, they are far from perfect, because, like all of us, they are human! They have quirks, faults, and needs, just like you and me. They change locations, groups, schools, and friends. If your whole life revolves around your gals, and you have a major fight or get betrayed or hurt by one of them, then your entire world will feel like it is crumbling down around you. Plus, friend-centered gals are way more likely to give into negative peer pressure and give up on their goals and dreams in order to "fit in."

Focusing on stuff you have control over, like your goals and dreams, is way healthier, and you'll end up with way better friendships because of it. Here's why:

- Nobody likes "cling-ons." People like to breathe and have room to do stuff on their own and with other friends. If you are friend-centered, your friends become your life, and you end up consulting with them over the tiniest little things—and expect them to do the same for you. If you don't "set them free," they might end up wanting out.
- Having your own interests makes you interesting and brings more to the table, giving you more to talk about and share with each other.
- You'll be way more confident and at ease with yourself, knowing you stand for something and believe in yourself. Not only will you feel great, you will be a great friend.

You might be friend-centered if:

- You call them to get their approval on whether you should wear your hair up or down—every day.
- You have a mini-meltdown if they even *think* about having lunch with somebody other than you.
- You can't imagine being without your cell phone for one second in case you miss one of their calls.
- You are referred to as the "cling-on," and you think it's cute.

Bottom line, ladies: whether you have one great friend or a hundred, don't make them the center of your universe. Real strength, confidence, and self-esteem come from the inside, not from your friends, as awesome as they are. But what if the roller coaster derails, or the ride comes to a sudden stop? Then what? Read on to find out how to deal with broken friendships—and how to fix them or end them and move on.

Friendship Rx

No matter how close you and your friends are, how far you go back, or how sure you are that the "BFF" you use to sign every note with will last forever, there are going to be times when your friendships are going to need a few repairs—or maybe end for good.

Growing Apart

When I was in elementary school, my best friend was a girl named Heather. We were born in the same hospital, two days apart. We grew up in the same town and went to school together. We were both smart and loved horses, and it seemed as if we were going to be friends forever. That also goes for Lisa, Amy, Nicole, Alisha, Amanda, Harbir, Mandy, and Crystal. I was really good friends with all these girls, and I thought we would always all hang out. Fast-forward to middle school—we all went our separate ways. I didn't ditch them, they didn't ditch me; we just grew apart. We started hanging out with different people, and some of us ended up moving away.

The point is that friendships change. People grow up, and sometimes they grow apart. It can be hard, especially if you feel like it's not your choice, but as the saying goes, when one door closes, another opens; you'll find another great group of gals. Nobody did anything wrong, and you'll always have the memories you shared together. I still get such a kick out of looking through old yearbooks and pictures. We had a great time together, and I'll always be grateful for growing up with such good friends.

If one of your pals isn't ready to give up the relationship, and you feel like you have moved on, it can be really painful for both of you. After all, the last thing in the world you want to do is hurt her. Now what? Try talking to her and explaining that as much as you love her as a person, you feel that you have outgrown each other and think it would be a good idea to find new friends. Explain that it doesn't mean you won't ever talk to her again; it's just that you feel like you need to spread your wings and think she should do the same.

Another common situation we all go through is doing something to screw up a friendship, either accidentally or on purpose. Don't worry; it doesn't mean your friendship is going down faster than the *Titanic*; there is still stuff you can do to fix it.

Not-So-Friendly Fights

"[In a fight]. I try to be the bigger person. There's no harm in saying. 'You know what? Whatever. I'm going to let it roll off.' I try to be generous with my response."
—Miley Cyrus

You are going to fight, get mad at each other, or be hurt or upset by something she does. It's normal; you both are dealing with a ton of stress; you are figuring yourselves out; and sometimes, people make mistakes.

Did you and your pal have a major blowout? Did you say some pretty hurtful stuff, and now she won't talk to you? Did she do the uber-shady thing of going behind your back and landing a date with your crush? Friendship meltdowns happen; we are all human, which means we are all gonna screw up now and again. The good news is that it's usually not the end of the world—or the friendship.

Here's how you can fix it:

- Try to understand *her* side of the story, and see if you can see where she is coming from. Maybe you guys can find some common ground?
- Talk about the problem. What did she do to hurt you? Why did it hurt you? How did it make you feel? What did you do to hurt her? How did it make her feel?
- Apologize if it was your fault. Tell her you are sorry; you didn't mean what you said (if it's true); you took stuff out on her that had nothing to do with her (which we often do with the people we love the most because we know they will be there for us); you were upset; or you lost your temper. Then, offer to do whatever it takes to make it up to her. Whatever you say, be sincere about it.
- If you were hurt, forgiveness comes in handy here. It doesn't mean you have to forget or get over it right away, but understand that we all make mistakes. And forgiveness is more about you, anyway; it's tough to go through life holding a grudge.
- Agree to take it slow if it was a big hurt, or plan a gal date to reconnect. And give it time—a little time does an amazing job of healing wounds.

But what about if one of you isn't ready to forgive and forget? It doesn't have to be the end of the world. (Remember, you are *you*-centered!) Here's how to tell if it's time to move on, for good.

When to End a Friendship

- You have been majorly burned, and you feel like there is no way you can ever feel comfortable trusting her again.
- One or both of you are not prepared to apologize or make the effort to be pals again.

- You were only friends because of the group or clique you were in, your boyfriends were friends, or there was some other "social" reason.
- You were friends from age two and have just grown apart.
- She did something really shady that makes you wonder what kind of person she really is.

Losing a friend can be really hard, even if it's a mutual decision. But there are some things you can do to cope:

- Give yourself permission to be upset; it's totally understandable and okay.
- Write a letter to her, telling her how you feel. Either give it to her, or burn it. Sometimes you'll feel better for just having written it out, so give it the "twenty-four-hour rule"—wait twenty-four hours after writing it, and then see if you still feel like sending it the next day.
- Reach out and make new friends, or strengthen the friendships you have. Plan a sleepover, or spend a day at the zoo, just having fun.
- Do some stuff for you, to connect with the inner you and feel better. Get a bouquet of flowers for your room, and spend an afternoon journaling or doing yoga.

Toxic Friends and Mean Girls

We've all met at least one. They are "friends" that seem to zap all your energy, require a whole *lot* of work, or make you feel like you work for them—and for what? Use these signs to spot a toxic friend before she leaves you exhausted and asking "What just happened?"

Toxic Friends: the Signs

- She is a major gossip. As soon as somebody is out of earshot, she starts ripping into her, trashing her on anything from her outfit or weight to her friends or grades. The chances are, if she's doing it *with* you, she'll do it *to* you as well.

- She can't take criticism. The great thing about a great friend is that you have somebody who will tell you the truth, no matter what. A toxic friend will only want to hear praise and compliments and will probably do the same for you. The trouble is, you never know where you really stand. It's easy to "buy" friends with compliments, but they usually don't last. If you try being honest with her, she'll probably freak out.

44

- She's super-concerned about her image. She has to look perfect all the time and takes herself way too seriously. If she can't laugh at herself or if she gets super-upset when somebody points out a flaw, then she's way too high maintenance for you.

- She's the Queen of Mean. People are scared to upset her because she could write *the* book on revenge.

- She's a "Cindi with an 'I'"; everything is "I, I, I"—all about her. That is not only totally draining, but it gets old fast. A real friend is just as concerned about listening to your problems as she is with telling you her own.

- She holds a grudge—forever! In the drama-filled world that is high school, grudges are pretty commonplace. But if you hurt or upset a friend, after some time has passed, and you've offered an apology and had a heartfelt discussion, she'll get over it and forgive you. A toxic friend won't, though—you have one shot, and if you do anything to lose your "friend" privilege, it's gone for good. Just ask Cathy—you know, the girl who had to transfer out of state because she liked toxic girl's old boyfriend.

- She doesn't support you. She likes to be the center of attention, and if you do anything to upstage her, it's on!

- She is dishonest or talks behind your back. Not cool.

- She pressures you into doing things you know you shouldn't—like drugs, alcohol, skipping school, or having sex. She needs an accomplice, and you usually feel way more stressed out after hanging with her than you do after hanging with your other friends.

- She brings you down. Her negativity drains all your energy, and you start to feel bad about yourself, confused, hurt, anxious, and unsure of yourself. If any of these describe a friend, then she is definitely a toxic friend, and it's time to find somebody who loves you, supports you, and values your friendship.

- She is one of the "cling-ons" mentioned earlier. It's super-important to have time to grow and nurture yourself and not have to baby-sit an overly needy pal.

If you ever feel like your "pal" makes you feel bad, treats you differently around different people, uses you, gossips about you, shares your secrets, drops you like a hot potato when she lands a guy, acts jealous of you, manipulates you, or is always putting you down, you have a plutonium pal—she's toxic! You need to distance yourself from her, pronto. Spend more time with other friends and slowly move apart from the toxic pal. It can be hard, especially if you want to "save" or "fix" her. Remember, it's not your responsibility to do that; it's hers.

Mean Girls

High school shouldn't make you feel like you are auditioning for *Mean Girls, the Sequel: Even Meaner.* We have all felt the wrath of cliques and mean girls. But who are these girls, and why do they have so much power? Here's what we know: 1) Mean girls exist. 2) They usually hunt in packs called "cliques." 3) Everybody equates the girls' meanness with popularity.

When I met mean girls in high school, it bothered me, of course, and sometimes it hurt. They didn't even know me, but they decided to not like me. Later, I found out it was because they were threatened by me and thought I was pretty and, therefore, competition. Girls work in weird ways sometimes. Try not to take it personally; it's more about them than you—in fact, it's all about them!

The thing about mean girls is that they usually have lower self-esteem than anybody else. Meanness is often rooted in pain, and the only way they know how to deal with it is to make other people feel as bad as they do. You feel bad; they feel powerful—mission accomplished.

"I go to a really big school, and there are two popular groups of girls. I used to be friends with the ringleader of one of them, but she totally turned her back on me when we went to high school. The only real problem was that she knew all my secrets and used them against me! She'd make fun of me in front of everyone, call me names, and torment me. One day, I was particularly stressed, and when I saw her coming, this fire boiled up inside me! She came over to me and started making fun of my outfit, and I totally stood up for myself—in front of everyone! It felt so good. And the best part is, to this day she never picked on me again!"
—Tanya, 17

When Enough Is Enough

If you seem to have a target on your chest for the mean-girl firing squad, you aren't doomed to a life of bullying; there are steps you can take, depending on what kind of mean girl you are dealing with.

- Set up a meeting with your teacher or principal and discuss what's going on. The chances are, you aren't the only one who feels like you do. You could even get a bunch of other girls together and have them come to the meeting, too, to discuss solutions.
- Talk to your mom and dad about it and see what they suggest.
- Try ignoring them totally; they might just get bored and leave you alone.
- Have a brainstorming session with your other pals who are at the mercy of these girls. Come up with a game plan, together. Maybe you'll agree to tell them how you feel; ignore them completely; set up a meeting with them, you guys, and a guidance counselor to try and work something out; or just act like they don't bother you at all—find something that works for you.
- Take one girl aside and try a heart-to-heart talk. They are a whole different animal when they are away from the pack, you might be surprised. The chances are she's not nearly as scary on her own, and she might not know the impact she's having on your life.
- Talk to a teacher about having a speaker or workshop leader come in to work on solutions.
- Organize a gal-to-gal day or a "Stop Bullying" campaign. (Go to www.empoweredgal.com to find out how.)
- If the bullying problem is a big one and nothing seems to help, check your state laws to see if you are in one of the twenty states that has laws against bullying, and look into pressing charges with the help of your family.

You can do more than just learn to deal with it. Stand up for yourself, however you are most comfortable. Nobody is going to stop it but you. The one thing mean girls think they have is power, but here's the thing—that power only works if you give it to them. If you are unsure of yourself or don't have much confidence, then their comments are totally going to rock you, because you might believe what they say. But if you own who you are and rock it, then the comments of some mean little girls aren't going to have the same impact on you. Don't let their words or actions get to you. Sure, those comments suck, but they don't—not at all—reflect who you are.

Ultimately, you can't change anybody, and sometimes, people are just mean, nasty, and unfriendly, no matter what. All you can do is change how you react to them, and how much you are going to let it get to you. Having a close group of pals helps, as does working on building your self-esteem. Focus on school, your friends, and the things that make you feel good. Ultimately, though, the only real cure for mean girls is for girls to get to know each other and to start seeing each other as sisters, not enemies. Take the opportunity to get to know the girls in your class, and show people how to treat you by how you treat them—and yourself.

You might be a mean girl if:

- You put other people down to feel good about yourself.
- You talk behind people's backs and gossip to bond with other girls.
- You drop people as friends to impress other friends.
- You judge people.
- You get jealous and act bitchy.
- You hide your insecurities by acting out.

Do any of those points fit you? It doesn't mean you are a bad person; it just means you have a lot of work to do. The things you say and do could really hurt somebody else, and you are way better than that. Want to stop being the Queen of Mean? Here's what you can do:
- Ditch the toxic friends and find new ones.
- Apologize. I know; it's hard, but if you know you've hurt somebody, say you are sorry and ask what you can do to make it up to her.
- Stop gossiping and talking behind people's backs. It's not cool, and it gives you a really bad rep.
- Think about the consequences of your actions.
- Find hobbies and interests to develop that'll help you feel better about yourself.

EG Tip: Don't be a "Gossip Girl." Just because the book is a best-seller doesn't mean that gossiping should be celebrated or tolerated. All it takes is breaking somebody's trust once for you to be labeled for the rest of your school career. Gossip sucks.

Avoiding "Popularitis"

Popularitis (noun): The desire to be popular at all costs.

I have to admit; I had a brush with "popularitis" in high school. I'd never been "popular," not in the traditional sense of the word, anyway. I had lots of friends; in fact, there weren't many people I wasn't friends with—except the popular clique. They tolerated me, and the girls were even friendly enough to me, one to one, but I never hung out with them. Fast-forward to the first move of my school career. I went from TinyTown to one slightly bigger, but in my mind, it was the Big League. (Hey, when you come from a town with more churches and cows than houses and people, anything with more than one street running through it is a big deal!) I decided I wanted to try to "fit in" in the traditional sense—I wanted to be popular! Being friends with everybody wasn't enough; I wanted to be "cool" and feel like I wasn't such an oddball. (I was the "different" one—that's how my mother introduced me, anyway!)

I spent the summer "cooling myself up." I added highlights to my hair—'cause as we all know, that's super-important—and I got a purse to (get this) *wear* in class, because that's what popular people did. I also got some cute little skirts, those sneakers that were oh so "in" at the time, and became an expert in makeup application. (I wanted to be a makeup artist back then, naturally.) Plus, I'd spent a summer in Cali, and that helped me really get it all down.

September rolled around, and I was ready. Cute outfit? Check. "It" shoes? Check. Hair and makeup? Check and check. Little purse? Check. I was set! I walked in there, where nobody knew me, and I rocked it. It took a good four months before I was "in" with the second-tier group. This was the highest I'd ever gotten—somebody pinch me! But the closer I got to the mean girls, who acted like they were the "queen bees," the more I understood what that "b" stood for. Yup, you guessed it. These weren't nice girls! They were mean, kind of skanky, and didn't care about school—*so* not me! The girls I was friends with were nice, and they felt the same way I did. The only problem was that they were suffering from popularitis, too.

They didn't realize that they were great people, and that true popularity meant being kind, nice, and friendly to *everyone*, not just the members of a clique. So, I chilled out a bit and started being myself, and I got even friendlier with the other groups. I started encouraging my pals to branch out, too, and I'd bring new girls or shy girls or "unpopular" girls to have lunch with us. I felt like a match-maker; people were totally opening their minds, and I am happy to report that by the end of the year, I was cured! I realized that being popular had nothing to do with being a bitch or being sorta slutty; it was all about being nice and treating people with respect. Nobody is better than anybody else, and I felt kind of silly that I'd gone to such lengths to be popular, especially when I was already popular, in the way that really mattered, just by being me.

That was a really great year for me. Most of the girls in my grade were getting along, and it was so much more fun. I was so happy to witness that and to find out that true popularity is a great thing. Being known for being nice and friendly is way better that being thought of as bitchy or nasty, even if it's only a handful of people who know you. And to this day, I don't understand how the meaner, nastier, and drama-queen girls were popular—that's an oxymoron, if you ask me! Just because those girls are pretty, date jocks, have expensive things, are on the cheerleading squad, or whatever else equals popularity at your school, it doesn't actually mean anything. Why? Because it's not real, and it doesn't last. Fast-forward to after graduation, and these chicks will have been taken down a peg or two, and we gals who were kind, nice, and friendly will have some wicked-awesome people skills—and we'll be thriving because of it. I actually feel bad for the mean girls because they have such a limited view of what's important, and they are missing out on a whole lot of great experiences by being so narrow-minded.

If you suffer from a raging case of popularitis, there is a cure. Start being your own girl, and keep these next few tips in mind:

- Know your value. Your self-worth depends on way more than being accepted by the popular girls, fitting in with a certain group or clique, or dating the popular guys. Even if you *are* one of those girls everybody wants to be, don't base who you are on who your friends are or on your social standing.
- Don't lose yourself. I know what it's like to want something so bad that you almost lose yourself in the process of achieving it. No matter what you are trying to get, always remain true to yourself. That's all you have, anyway, especially after high school is over. Sure, some of your friends might go to the same college as you, but once you are out in the real world—or at least the college world—you are going to have to stand on your own two feet and use skills and lessons you (hopefully) picked up in high school.

- Develop your interests. If you love soccer, football, drama, or art, keep it up. Focus on your passion, and challenge yourself to be the best you can be. Plus, you are more likely to find friends who like you for *you* and who share common interests if you do stuff you love. Plus, you'll be *way* happier, too, which is a bonus, right?
- Be open to making new friends. The problem with shutting yourself off in a clique or trying to fit in with a certain group is that you are not giving yourself the opportunity to explore other friendships and meet new people who could open your mind and share new opportunities and experiences with you. I don't know about you, but I'd rather be friends with a bunch of different people who challenge me in different ways and motivate me to be my best, than with a group of girls who are exactly the same.
- Think for yourself. The trouble with getting caught up in a certain group or clique is that you stop thinking for yourself and instead, you go along with the group consensus. Think about how you feel about certain things, develop a good moral and value system, and think for yourself about what is right and what is wrong. If you see something that you feel is wrong, speak up.
- Labels schmabels. So what if you're considered a "nerd" or a "drama geek"? The nerds grow up to be billionaires, and the drama geeks grow up to win Oscars and own houses all over the world. The trouble with mean girls is that they peak in high school. It's the only environment where they can excel. Think about it: Where else will people tolerate that behavior? The only place they have a captive audience, where they can "rule" and get away with it, is in high school. That kind of stuff gets old—fast— in the real world.
- Have really big goals and dreams. People often tell me that I should be on the Oprah show—which would be *awesome*—but I tell them that my goal isn't just to be on the *Oprah* show; my goal is to have Oprah on *my* show! Having mega-big goals, staying me-centered, and focusing on something I really loved made dealing with all the friend drama (and everything else) so much easier in high school. Set some mega-goals for yourself, and do something every day to get closer to reaching them.

"I want people to love me. but it's not going to hurt me if they don't."
—Drew Barrymore

Gal to Gal

"Have one evening a week or every other week where you and your friends get together and do something fun, like a weekly friendship ritual. My best friends and I get together to watch The Hills every Monday, and we cook snacks and read magazines. It's really fun to just chill out together."
—Julia, 15

"Put into a relationship what you want to get out of it."
—DeDe, 16

"Love [your friends] for who they are, not who you want them to be."
—Kayla, 17

"Be supportive of each other. High school is tough, so be there for each other during the ups and downs."
—Kate, 20

"Have fun! Friends should have fun together; don't take it too seriously."
—Laquisha, 16

Hey, it's okay to:

- Have made mistakes in the past about friends; just start over.
- Be between friends at the moment (and take applications for new ones! :-)).
- Have a ton of friends, have a couple friends, or to prefer to hang with the boys.
- Find drama-free friends and skip the roller coaster all together if you can!

Stick around for Lesson 3. It's all about building a win/win relationship with your parents, how to get more of what you want and less of what you don't, and how to deal if things aren't perfect at home.

Lesson 3:
Parents 101

Whether or not your mom and dad get along and are still married, can't stand each other and are divorced, fight all the time, are partially or full-time absent from your life, show their love for you, yell at you, are messed up, or just plain crazy, you no doubt have some kind of issues with your parents. We all do; nobody's family is perfect, even if it looks that way from the outside. But whatever your 'rent situation, there are about a million ways to make it better—you can have it work for you, have them treat you like an adult, get closer to them, get their support, and live in a more peaceful environment. Cool? I thought so!

"Parents can only give good advice or put [children] on the right paths, but the final forming of a person's character lies in [his] own hands."

—Anne Frank (advice from her father in *The Diary of Anne Frank*)

You might be wondering why the relationship with your parents is such a big deal. You spend at least the first eighteen years of your life with them. They are the gatekeepers to your freedom and social life. They are the ones who are there through thick and thin and will be supporting you through college. You don't really grow apart from them, as you do with friends and boyfriends. In fact, you grow closer as you grow up and you see that hey, maybe they weren't so bad, after all! (You can stop rolling your eyes—it's true!)

They are going to be the ones walking you down the aisle, burping your babies, and carving the turkey with you and *your* family for years and years to come. Whether you like it or not, they are going to be around, so you have a choice. You can either have a healthy, loving, supportive relationship that works great for both of you, or you can keep thinking they are aliens about to return to the mother ship at any moment and have a less than stellar relationship.

Sometimes, though, families aren't the safe havens we hope for. They may cause us a ton of pain, and no matter how much we try, we just can't fix what has been broken through no fault of our own. Sometimes, parents go away and never come back; sometimes they do awful things to us; sometimes they leave all too soon, and we feel lost and alone in the world. Whatever your parental situation, there is hope. You can either do your part to make your relationship better, or you can surround yourself with a "family" you make for yourself, with friends and mentors. But before we get going, let's try another IQ quiz.

What's Your Parent IQ?

1 = No way; **2** = Sorta, sometimes; **3** = Sure do!

1) I have a great relationship with my parents.	1	2	3
2) My parents support me and my goals and dreams.	1	2	3
3) My parents trust me.	1	2	3
4) I treat my parents with respect.	1	2	3
5) I help out around the house and do my chores.	1	2	3
6) I know what's going on in my parents' lives.	1	2	3
7) My 'rents know what's going on in my life.	1	2	3
8) I feel comfortable telling my parents how I feel.	1	2	3
9) I feel like my parents love me, no matter what.	1	2	3
10) I love my parents, no matter what.	1	2	3

Now add up the numbers and find your Parental IQ. **Total:**_____

Scoring:

10-15: If your score falls in this range, your parental situation might be a little rough. Whether you have parents who are absent from your life, or are abusive or whatever the case may be, this chapter will help you understand what's going on and help you find ways to repair the situation, or create a family of your own—because it can get better.

16-22: Some parts of the relationship are great; some parts are not so great, which is totally normal. You may not feel as close to your parents as you'd like, and maybe you wish they knew you a little better, too. You can find out how to change all that and work towards a healthy, strong, loving relationship with them, which would be cool, right?

23-30: Sounds like you and your family could star in your very own feel-good family sitcom! Still, that doesn't mean there aren't issues here and there, so read on to uncover some tips and strategies for making a good relationship even better.

Everyone has a unique relationship with their parents, kind of like a fingerprint. Some are great, some are good, some are just fine, and others are not so great at all. No matter which category you and your family fit into, you aren't alone, and there are things you can start doing today to make it better. In "Understanding Your 'Rents," I'll talk about trying to see your parents' point of view (POV), figuring out where they come from, and getting on the same page. Then, in "Building a Win/ Win Relationship," I'll cover what you can do to help build a better relationship alongside your parents. You'll learn some communication techniques, how to make time for your family in your ka-razy life, how to get the most from your relationship, and how to start getting the responsibility you want. And the last section, "Parent Rx," is for you gals with a less than stellar family life. You'll learn how you can forgive and start repairing a damaged situation, or deal with sucky situations and build your own families with friends and mentors.

Understanding Your 'Rents

"My parents used to be so annoying, and I honestly thought they were out to get me. But now that I'm older, I can see that they really do love me and care about me ... and they aren't out to get me at all!"
—Allison, 18

"Sometimes I know I'm not very nice to my mom and dad. When I get stressed, I take it out on them. I feel bad, but I think they understand."
—Danielle, 14

"My mom left when I was little because of her drinking problem, so my dad had to raise me and my little sister. It's hard, and I wonder who [my mom] is and if she thinks about me. But I am grateful for my dad."
—Alex, 15

"I have a good relationship with my mom and dad. We get on really well, and because I help out around the house and am trustworthy, they let me do more stuff than my friend's parents let them do. It's pretty cool!"
—Arielle, 16

It sucks to wake up one day and realize your parents aren't perfect. When we are little, our parents seem to do no wrong. Then at some point, usually sooner than later, we see that they are, in fact, human. Unfortunately, we begin to see them as Martians soon after that, and we spend most of our teen years trying to decode their language.

As I said earlier, everybody has a different relationship with their parents, so all I'm going to do here is offer tips and advice on how to make your relationship better. You might feel that you have the capacity to create a great relationship with your parents, if you don't, it's somehow your fault—that feeling is totally normal, but feeling that way doesn't mean it's true. Sometimes, no matter what you do, your parents can't or won't provide the nurturing relationship that you need—they are human and sometimes have a ton of issues of their own. Or maybe you are one of the thousands of kids in foster care and have been in more homes than you care to remember. For our purposes in this section, however, I'm going to assume that you have relatively normal parents and that a healthy relationship is possible. If that doesn't apply to you, pay extra attention to the last part of this lesson, where you will find a ton of tips and advice on how to live a happy, healthy, "normal family life," in spite of your actual family!

And remember, nobody has a perfect relationship with their parents. The ones you see on TV aren't real! Have realistic expectations. Your parents are your parents, they are who they are, and it's unfair on them *and* to you to wish they were different.

Note: I know the words "mom" and "dad" mean different things to different people. If your aunt, uncle, grandma, grandpa, big brother, big sister, neighbor, other legal guardian, or some combination of the above is raising you, just substitute that in for "mom" or "dad." Whoever your parents may be, if you love them and they love you, that's what makes a family.

What to Know about Your 'Rents

I am not a parent, but I have a dog. She is my (fur) baby. I love her so much, and it's crazy how much I worry about her. I want her to be happy, safe, and protected, and to one day grow up and go to Harvard. Wait … what? Never mind the last part, but I assume that is how most parents feel about their kids—times about a billion. Kind of freaks me out to think I could love and worry so much about something, but parents do, about you, every single day. No wonder they are kind of cranky sometimes and freak out when your curfew goes whizzing by and they haven't got a call! Check below for some things you need to know about your 'rents. (It's true for most of them—the "normal" ones, anyway!)

- They love you—lots—even if you don't think they do.

- They want what they think is best for you.

- It's really hard for them when they no longer feel needed as you grow up and become more independent.

- They worry about what you really are up to, imagining the worst.

- They think you can do better, especially when it comes to school, friends, and guys—especially guys. (That will never change!)

- They don't "get" the music you listen to, the clothes you wear, why you want to be the next American Idol, or what LMAO, LOL, or TTYL means, but they imagine it's something really, *really* bad.

- They *want* to trust you, be friends with you, and give you the freedom you want.

- They make mistakes. Sometimes big ones. Sometimes, really big ones.

- They are probably trying really hard and have a ton on their plate, everything from finances to how they are going to make it to your track meet on Tuesday.

Your parents are usually carrying a pretty huge load trying to make it all work, keep you happy, do what's best for you, and still try to have a life of their own. You need to understand that you and your parents disagree (don't pretend you don't) because you have different points of view. They are stressed about money, their jobs, taking care of the home and the garden, car payments, cooking dinner, trying to raise a productive member of society, making sure you are safe, having what you need, and hoping that you stay out of trouble—plus trying to make their own relationships work. You stress about your friends, looks, tests, homework, boys, clothes, mean girls, college, figuring out who you are, what you want to do with your life, and finding your own voice.

Both situations are pretty stressful, but they are different, and that's where the conflict usually springs from. It's tough to find common ground, but it's really worth the effort once you do. And the cool thing is, even though you and your parents are going through such different stuff, the one thing that you both have in common is wanting a win/win relationship. Here's how to get one:

Building a Win/Win Relationship

Who doesn't want a super-awesome relationship with her parents? I know I did, growing up, but one of my parents didn't want a super-awesome relationship with me! My dad did; he is still one of my best friends. My mother, on the other hand, didn't, and to this day doesn't want a relationship with me or my sister. But I realized that I couldn't change her, as much as I wanted to, and that I could feel complete in knowing that I acted in the best, most loving way I could, given the circumstances. I would fantasize about having a great relationship with my mother, and the things I came up with are the things that pretty much all teens want. Here's what a win/win relationship looks like:

- You love and support each other and enjoy each other's company.
- You and your parents communicate openly and honestly but keep certain things private, too.
- You feel that you can talk to your 'rents about anything, and they know they can confide in you as well.
- You enjoy spending time with them but give them space (as they do for you) for their own interests, hobbies, and "me time."
- You solve problems and get through hard times together.
- You are willing to work on making the relationship a win/win.

Now, that is a best-case scenario, but if you're not there yet, you and your family can take steps to get there.

Get on the Same Page

Are you and your parents on the same page? Before you can take steps to build a great relationship, you need to know what is going on in each other's lives and how you both feel. It's important to get on the same page as your 'rents, and let them know how you feel about them and the relationship. Now, if your family doesn't communicate well, the following suggestion might be hard to do, but it's worth it to try.

First of all, pick a time when your parents aren't crazy-busy, and ask if they have a sec to chat. Then, saying something like this usually does the trick:

"Hey Mom and Dad, I have been thinking a lot about our relationship, and I want us to be on the same page. I just want you to know that even though we fight, and I have been spending more time with my friends and

stuff lately, I really do appreciate everything you guys do for me. I'd really like to do my part to make this relationship better for both of us and even get to know you a little better."

Add stuff that is true for you. Maybe you want to apologize for some bad decisions you've made, or maybe you want to spend more time together. Whatever it is, just be open and honest. You really don't have a lot to lose. And ask them what they'd like you to know, too, or what steps they think you all could take to make it a win/win relationship. It's a great starting-off point. If they aren't sure, ask them to think about it, and maybe you could talk about it later on.

The point of this is to provide a clean slate that you can all start building on. Speaking of which …

Building Blocks

In any relationship, you can do things to add to it and make it better, or take away from it and make it worse. Here is a list of things you can do to start building a great relationship:

> **Building Block 1:** Instead of blowing off family time to hang with your friends, show your family that they mean a lot to you by opting for quality time with them.

> **Building Block 2:** Pop in to see Mom or Dad at work every once in a while, if that's okay. Say hi to their fellow employees, and offer to lend a hand with filing or licking stamps or something. It's a great way to get work experience and an even better way to learn what your mom or dad deals with on a daily basis.

> **Building Block 3:** Take the load off. If your mom is running late, offer to pick up your li'l sis from school or get dinner started. Small stuff like that goes a long way, and your parents will likely return the favor down the road.

> **Building Block 4:** Keep your room clean, take out the trash, do the dishes, and keep up on your chores. Believe it or not, your mom doesn't like nagging you; she just does it because she has to!

> **Building Block 5:** Start a new ritual: a morning or evening walk together, even if you don't have a

dog! It's a great way to stay fit and get to know each other in a low-key kind of way.

Building Block 6: Do a mom/daughter, dad/daughter, or family book club. Take turns picking the book, and each day, at breakfast or dinner, talk about what you think about it.

Building Block 7: Start your own family game night. Pick a night you are usually all at home and take turns choosing the game to play that evening.

Building Block 8: Be thoughtful. Does your mom love roses or some kind of ornaments? Surprise her with her favorite things on her birthday, Mother's Day, or just because! Same goes for your dad, too.

Building Block 9: Be polite. This one may seem like a no-brainer, but it goes such a long way. Saying please and thank you and being nice to your parents' friends will make them so proud of you, and they will soon start to see you as the adult you are becoming.

Building Block 10: Make up after a fight. Say you are sorry, and accept their apology, too. There is no point holding grudges or letting things get out of control.

Get to Know 'Em

Believe it or not, your parents aren't freaky alien creatures, and can, on occasion, be kind of cool. The catch is, you've got to get to know them first. Here's how:

- Ask them questions about their childhoods, their hopes and dreams, their worries, what they love about their life, etc. Share your answers, too.
- Look over old photo albums together, and share memories.
- Ask to spend a day doing stuff together, just hanging out and talking.
- Explore their interests with them, like golf or old movies. Invite them to do stuff you love with you, too.
- Do one random, fun thing together each week, like going to an art gallery, getting a makeover at the makeup counter, watching a sports event, etc.

Invite Them into Your World

I am willing to bet that your parents would like to get to know you a little better, too. You are going through about a million changes right now, and your parents are probably just as confused as you are, especially if you are the oldest child, and they haven't gone through the teen years with any of your siblings. By inviting them into your world, just a bit, they'll get to see that it's not such a scary place, and they will get to know the awesome gal you are a whole lot better. Try some of these ideas to get the ball rolling:

- Invite your mama out to see the latest teen flick that you are dying to see. Watching it together will be a great bonding experience, and she'll get a little insight into what you are going through.

- Invite them to chat with you and your friends for a while, or hang out in the kitchen and have everybody pitch in to help make dinner. They'll get to know everybody better and see what your life is like.

- Talk to them about your life, if you have that kind of relationship. Tell them what's going on and the latest news from your high-school halls.

- Let your mom and dad read this book to get a better idea of what you are dealing with.

Now that you guys have a better understanding of each other, there are still a couple things standing between you and freedom. Getting your parents' trust is huge and is a really important step on the road to maturity. The good news? It's not that hard to get, but gaining it back after you have lost it is a whole lot harder. So, once you have it, hold onto it, and if you've lost it, it's time to put in the necessary work to get it back.

Gaining Your 'Rents' Trust

Have you ever been grounded? Had your car keys taken away? Been made to miss out on parties with your friends? What if I told you that by mastering a few simple techniques, you'll never have to deal with these less-than-fun situations again? Sounds good, right?

You may think your parents are strict and totally unfair. But as hard as it is, take a look and see what your role was and is in the situation. Maybe they don't trust you or are "unfair" because:

- You lied about where you were, who you were with, and what you were doing.
- They caught you sneaking in, sneaking out, or stealing the car for the evening.
- You always come in later than your curfew.
- You answer with "nothing" and "nowhere" when they ask you what you were doing and where you where.
- You never do anything for them without being asked a million times.
- You don't show any interest in their lives, how they feel, or what they do for you.
- The only time you speak to them is to argue, ask for something, or when you need their help to bail you out.
- Your friends are super-shady and known for getting trouble.
- You can't take no for an answer, and act like a child (with or without a temper tantrum) when you are disciplined.

If any those are true for you, do you get why your 'rents might be a little freaked out about lending you the car on Saturday night? Or maybe your parents are strict or super-protective by nature. Whatever it may be, gaining your parents' trust is key if you want any kind of freedom! So, what do you do? You need to start showing them that you are a responsible adult, which is how you want to be treated, right? Like all things worth having, you have to earn it.

Talk to your parents. Tell them about your day instead of responding with the classic "I don't know" or "Nothing." That makes them think you are keeping secrets, and you only keep secrets about things you don't want them to know. Even if you were innocently shopping away the afternoon, your dear old dad is picturing orgies with rock stars, massive quantities of drugs, and … well, you get the picture. By talking to them, they feel reassured and trusting of you. Voila! You are on the road to freedom already!

Be honest. If you get caught doing something you shouldn't, or you lie about something, it's going to take a lot to undo, so instead, be honest—even if it's hard. It's cliché, but honesty really is the best policy, and parents appreciate it.

Keep your grades up. If your mama and papa see that you are responsible in other areas of your life, they'll see that you can be responsible when it comes to choosing friends and boyfriends, social activities, and making grown-up decisions. By putting in the extra time and effort to maintain good grades, it's one less thing for your parents to worry about.

Do stuff for them. Whether it is unloading the dishwasher, or taking out the trash without being asked, or offering to pick up your little brother from baseball practice, which shows your parents that you care about them and making their lives easier, they'll be way more willing to do the same for you.

Be consistent. Remember that time that you said you were going to the library and actually went to a concert—and got caught? Yeah, don't do that. That gives your parents a reason to worry about you. They wonder why you have to lie and what you are hiding. They feel like they can't trust you. Just because you know that you are safe and fine doesn't mean they will know that. If you want to be treated like an adult, be up front, and do what you say you're going to do. This shows them you are responsible and mature and have integrity. If you are responsible, then they will treat you accordingly.

Surround yourself with positive people: If you are hanging out with a thirty-four-year-old biker, your chances of getting a later curfew—or even being allowed out the house, for that matter—are pretty slim. One of my mentors, Jack Canfield (*Chicken Soup for the Soul)* talks about how you are the average of the five people you spend the most time with, so look at your average. Do you parents have a right to be a little freaked out? Also, make sure your friends treat your parents with respect. If Sara has an attitude and is rude to your mom, no matter how cool she is with you, you are going to have a problem.

Make them feel needed. Even if you don't think you need your parents for stuff, let them feel like they still matter in your world. Ask your dad to help you fix your bike tire, or have your mom braid your hair. Including them in your day-to-day life, so they still feel useful and needed, will mean a lot and will show them that you are mature enough to ask them for help. That way, they feel that if one day you really do need help, you'll come to them.

It can be hard for your parents to see you as an adult and treat you accordingly. To them, you are still the toddler that they baby-proofed the house for—except now, they are trying to baby-proof the entire world. Not an easy task. But when they start to see that you are mature, responsible, honest, and capable of taking care of yourself, not only are they going to treat you like the adult you are becoming, but they are also probably going to give you more freedom as well.

Know Your Parents' Buttons—and Don't Push 'Em!

Who hasn't heard "You are really pushing my buttons right now!"? It's straight out of the parent playbook! But, ladies, you can use it to your advantage. One thing I used to do—and it always drove my parents nuts—was leaving my stuff laying around. They would always nag at me, and eventually, my mother would pick up my stuff, stick it in a bag, and throw it outside. I'd get so mad! But then I realized something: if I picked up my stuff—without being told—that was one less conflict. I knew that if I pressed that button (being messy), I'd get the same result (nagging and having my stuff tossed out), which wasn't any fun for anybody. So, ask yourself what you are doing that might be pushing your parents' buttons.

Check the following examples. You could be causing conflict between you and your parents, if you:

- Don't take out the trash.
- Keep your room messy.
- Charge up huge phone bills.
- Lie around the house.
- Don't pick up your stuff
- Talk back.
- Are lazy.
- Fight with your li'l bro or sis.
- Don't take the dog for a walk.
- Stay up too late.
- Watch too much TV.
- Don't do your homework.

If you are pushing your parents' buttons but wondering why they are nagging, bickering, or getting frustrated with you, change your ways. Walk the dog, do the dishes, take the trash out. It doesn't take much effort, but it goes a long way. Plus, once you start avoiding the negative buttons, you can start pushing the buttons that get you what you want.

"My mom would always be so happy when I'd cook dinner. She works two jobs. and would do anything for my sister and me. and never has any time for herself. She'd come home from work. make dinner. help us with our homework. tidy up. and then go to bed. I started taking cooking as an elective in ninth grade. and started cooking dinner and having dinner ready when she got home. It meant so much to her. and she really appreciated it. She saw me as being more of an adult. and she gave me more freedom because of it."
—Alyssa, 17

As Alyssa shows us, by doing things that make our parents happy—pushing the right buttons—it's a win/win. Her mom was happy that she didn't have to cook dinner every night and had some time to relax, and Alyssa got more freedom because she showed her mom how responsible and thoughtful she was.

The right buttons to push:

- Trying really hard at school
- Picking up the groceries
- Baby-sitting your siblings
- Cleaning up the house
- Cooking dinner
- Clearing the table
- Walking the dog
- Doing things without being asked
- Offering to help
- Reading a book or doing homework instead of watching TV
- Inviting your mom to chat with you and your friends
- Telling the truth

"My mom is incredible. I always listen to her. ... We're best friends. and at the same time we'll butt heads every now and then because we have the exact same personality."
—Ashlee Simpson

Communication: A Good Thing

I can't tell you how important communication is. Hold on—maybe I can. Communication is super-important—there! Why? Well, remember how we talked about how you and your parents are coming from two totally different points of view? It's really important to discuss things with them so you stay on the same page. Plus, sometimes big, bad, or confusing things happen, and your parents are the only ones you can talk to. So, where do you start? It depends on what kind of relationship you have, but here are some general tips:

Have a plan. Know what it is that you want to say and how you want to say it. It's a good idea to have a general idea of what you want to get out of the discussion, but it's important not to have super-high expectations, because you might not get exactly what you want from them. Whether you want to talk about getting a later curfew, your plea to start dating, help with something, borrowing the car, or your future, go over some of the main points you want to make—in your head or out loud, by yourself—before you actually speak with them.

Some Convo Starters:
- "A friend of mine at school (insert problem or experience here). What do you think about that?"

- "When you were my age, what kinds of things did you have to deal with?"

- "I'm having a problem with (insert your problem here). Do you have any advice?"

- "How do you feel about the election (the war, current events, my haircut, etc.)?"

Pick a good time. You don't want to bring up something as they rush off to work, come home from work, are cooking dinner, or are super-stressed out. Pick a time when you and your parents are relaxing or hanging out. If that is pretty rare, then set up a time in the near future. As you leave for school one morning, tell them you have something you'd like to talk about, and ask if you could set aside some time in the next couple of days to sit down and discuss it.

How to Get Your Point Across—the EG Way!

Even in you get on great with your parents, you still aren't going to see eye to eye with them on everything. You are going to have different feelings, opinions, and ideas than they do. You may feel something is unfair, but your parents may feel they are completely justified in their actions. So, what do you do? You could either storm up to your room and sulk for the next three months, or you could put on your big-girl panties and try the following:

Stay calm. Getting all upset and letting your emotions get the better of you is just cause for disaster. Take some deep breaths, stay calm, and collect yourself.

Don't accuse. Remember the "I" sentences from elementary school? ("I am hurt and upset about___" instead of "You totally ruined my life!") They come in handy here, too. Don't accuse your parents of anything. Comments like "You are so unfair! You just don't get it! I can't take living here with you anymore!" aren't going to get you anywhere. Instead, try something like, "I feel like I am responsible and mature enough to handle this, and this is why ..." See how that might work better?

Keep an open mind. Even though you *totally* don't agree with them, at least listen to their concerns and how they feel. By showing them some respect, they'll show you respect in return. But if you are feeling especially mature, why not try to put on their glasses for a sec, and see the situation through their eyes. Once you do that, you might just see that they actually do have a point, and you will be better able to come to some sort of common ground.

Accept the result. Even if you don't end up getting what you want, accept it like an adult. Remember, like all relationships, it's give and take. Don't storm off, get super-upset, or start having a fit. And don't beg, either. Not cool. Instead, look them in their eyes and say, "I respect your decision, and if you choose to change your mind about this in the future, I'll be happy to work on a compromise we can both be happy with." Make sure you accept their decision on an internal level, too, because you might start harboring resentment towards them, which could undo all your hard work.

Pick your battles. Every once in a while, let your parents "win" when they are expecting a fight. This shows maturity and respect for their opinion. If it's not a huge deal—if you are only asking because your friends are pressuring you to or you have something bigger you want to negotiate later—you might want to let this one slide. Your parents might just return the favor by letting you do something that is more important to you anyway, with little or no fight.

EG Tip: If you are really angry at your mom and dad and want to tell them so, make sure you invoke the "Twenty-Four–Hour" rule we talked about earlier—to make sure you still feel the same way the next day!

Parent-Approved Sayings

Master these little babies, and you will be in your parents' good books in no time!
- "I love you."
- "How can I help with this?"
- "What can I do to make it better (easier) for you?"
- "I'm sorry. What can I do to make it up to you?"
- "It's okay; I forgive you."
- "Thank you."
- "Okay, I'll do it."
- "I'd love to help, Dad, but I have a million hours of homework. Can I do it later?"
- "Sure. You need anything else while I'm out?"
- "Let me take care of dinner (picking up Kelly from school, cleaning the house, doing the dishes, walking the dog, etc.)."

But avoid saying anything like this:
- "I hate you!" (You probably don't mean it, anyway.)
- "Um … how about no?"
- "I'm too busy; why can't you do it?"
- "You *should* be sorry!"
- "I'm running away, quitting school, and marrying that guy out front with all the tats on the Harley that he stole earlier today. See ya!"

See, it's not so hard to communicate effectively. Show this lesson to your 'rents, and use it as a starting point for the way you interact.

But what if there is some stuff going on at home that is pretty tough, like arguing, name-calling or whatever? The following is for you. Here's how to deal:
- Have a family meeting. In our house, we used a piece of wood (or a mop, pen, cat, or whatever else was on hand) as the "speaker stick," and only the person holding the stick could talk. That way, people weren't yelling over each other to be heard, and everybody had a fair shot to express themselves.

- Tell your parents how it makes you feel when they yell and shout at you or each other. Use "I" sentences, like "I feel really insecure and sad when you yell at me."

- Keep a piece of paper on the fridge, where you can write your name down for that week's family meeting to talk about something.

- Find ways to blow off steam if listening to your 'rents fighting is driving you nuts. Go for a jog; turn the tunes up real loud to drown them out; have a super-long, super-hot, super-bubbly bath; head to your friends for a chill-out chat; or join a gym and beat up a punching bag.

- If you guys are always arguing or conflicting, there are a million (I counted) family counseling services in the phone book. Some may be through your church or community center, and others are private practices. Either way, there is one that will work great for your family, financially and—more important—emotionally. There is no shame in getting help and trying to make your family situation better.

Parental Rx

We've all said stuff we regret, and I'm no exception. Our words have a lasting effect, and they hurt. But no matter what actions and words have affected your relationship, it's never too late to start repairing the damage. The chances are, unless your parents are the not-so-great ones we talked about earlier, they want to have a great relationship with you, too. I asked some parents about what they wanted most out of their relationships with their daughters, and this is what they said:

"I mostly just want for my daughter and I to see eye to eye on things."
—Marleen

"I guess I just want [us] to start communicating."
—Jann

"Well. I want us to forgive each other and move forward."
—Doug

The chances are, your mom and pop want the same things, too. So, no matter how far down the wrong track you are, you can still find your way back to where you want to be. Here's how:

Forgive them. Has your mom been super-hard on you? Has your dad been working too hard? Are your parents split up or arguing all the time? Do they take their anger out on you? Going through life holding a grudge is like dragging a hundred-pound weight around with you wherever you go. It's tiring! Find it in your heart to forgive your parents for the human mistakes they have made. Remember, they are people, too. I'm not saying that you have to condone it; I'm just saying you need to forgive them—for you. Even if they are no longer in your life, forgiveness is always about you. I forgave my mom—not for her sake, not because I think she's changed—because I couldn't live my life blaming her or being angry at her. What's done is done, and the only person responsible for my life is me, so after a while, I managed to forgive her, and I encourage you to do the same, when you are ready.

Forgive yourself. Did you go through a rough patch? Did you do drugs? Lash out at your parents? Put yourself at risk? If you went through anything that put a strain on your family relationship, it's okay to forgive yourself, too.

Take it slow. If things have been rough for the past couple of years, it's unfair to you and your parents to expect things to change overnight. Make an effort to do something every day to make it better and build a new relationship.

Sucky Situations

Having parents who fight all the time, who seem to hate you or the other partner, who yell and scream, who are physically or mentally abusive, who freak out over the smallest things and make you feel like a nobody—these are the worst things that can happen to a kid. I know; I went through all that—and then some—with my mom as I was growing up. I'm not ashamed to say it, because I know millions of other people go through the same thing, and it has made me the person I am today. If you are living in a situation like that right now, I know exactly what you are going through. But I made it out just fine, and you can, too. Here's what you need to know:

- It is absolutely, positively *never* your fault. Ever. If one or both of your parents is mentally unwell, addicted to drugs or alcohol, or is just one of those crazy people, you did nothing to deserve it or bring it on.
- It is super-important to have an adult to talk to. I had my dad and a couple teachers at school who helped me so much. Don't be afraid to reach out and ask for help, even if it's just somebody to talk to.

- If the situation is physically or sexually abusive, you *must* get out right away. Tell somebody you trust, and have him or her call social services to get you out of that house. It's scary and a huge step, but if you don't stop it, nobody else will. It takes a ton of courage, but if you have siblings in that environment, you need to speak up for them as well.
- Try to get help for your parents if they are sick in some way. Talk to them, tell them how you feel, and ask them to go to therapy, take their medication, go to the doctor, or enroll in AA or drug rehab. If they won't, look into moving in with a family member or friend until it is safe to return home.
- Break the cycle. It can end with you, and it doesn't mean that you have to repeat your parents' mistakes. Get counseling or therapy, if needed, and turn it into something positive. When you are ready, write about it and share your story. Knowing it could help others will help you to deal with it a whole lot better.
- If you don't feel that you can talk to anyone you know about your situation, at the very least call the National Child Abuse Hot Line (1-800-25-ABUSE) or go online to www.ChildHelpUSA.com. There are tons more resources and info out there for you, so check it out.

No matter what kind of sucky situation you or your family is in, the only thing you can control is you—your actions and your decisions. It's not your responsibility to raise your parents and give up your teenhood trying to make them better. If they won't help themselves, there is nothing you can do. I know that is super-hard to grasp, and I wish I would have gotten that sooner—*way* sooner. Usually, when a parent is dealing with drugs, alcohol, or addiction, he or she is cruising down a long, lonely river called denial. Try to talk to other family members, or call a helpline (1-800-25-ABUSE) and ask for advice. It's hard, I know. Some people repeat the patterns from their own childhoods and don't know there is another option, but I'm telling you: there is an option. You can build your own support system of friends and healthy family members, and work your way towards an understanding and—hopefully, one day—forgiveness.

"Life is very interesting. In the end, some of your greatest pains become your greatest strengths."
—Drew Barrymore

As you can see, parental relationships can be beyond confusing, but they can also be a great source of comfort and support. Like any relationship, it takes work on all sides, but with a little effort, a touch of forgiveness and understanding, and a whole lot of love, you, too, can enjoy a win/win relationship with your mom and dad or whoever makes up your family.

Gal to Gal

"It's simple. If you want [parents] to treat you like a responsible grown-up, act like one!"

—Monique, 14

"Trust [your parents]. They usually have really good answers and advice if you just listen or ask for it."

—Sara, 15

"Remember that [parents] are people too, and they make mistakes. Forgive each other."

—Carly, 16

"Talk to them! Even if it's just about nothing—you know, like the weather. It'll mean something to them."

—Jennifer, 16

"Be nice! So many of my friends are so mean to their parents, and then they wonder why they are getting in so much trouble. Say please and thank you, listen to them, don't yell or name call. My mom is my best friend, and I couldn't imagine saying some of those things to her!"

—Mattie, 17

Hey, it's okay to:

- Have misunderstandings and arguments—you're human!
- Be friends with your parents (but make sure you are parent and daughter first, friends second).
- Have secrets and stuff you don't tell them. It's healthy!
- Grow up and become independent—you are supposed to!
- Create your own family with friends, relatives, friends' families, and other people you love, to get the support and love you need and deserve.

- Stay tuned for Dating Gal 101. It's filled with some pretty wicked dating advice and some insider info you won't want to miss. By the end of it, you will be a dating expert, understand guys a whole lot better, know how to master a first date (and land a second), and get what you need outta the relationship. Oh, and you'll see why being single is just as awesome as being coupled, so don't stress!

Lesson 4:
Dating Gal 101

It was tempting to leave this entire chapter blank, because I don't think anyone actually understands guys and dating at all! Just kidding—it may seem like that in high school, but as complicated as it seems, it's actually not that bad. It's just new, and it's a whole different game from "dating" in third grade or being friends with guys. There is a ton of emotions, feelings, and … ahem … hormones involved that make it all sound pretty darn complex. And I'm not gonna lie; it sometimes is. Dating in high school is sorta like being on a soap opera, except without the stuffy wardrobe and "evil twins." But it is totally within your grasp to figure it all out and make the best decisions for you, no matter what your evil twin is up to.

"The man for me is the cherry on the pie. But I'm the pie. and my pie is good all by itself. Even if I don't have a cherry."
—Halle Berry, actress

Let's get one thing straight: *You don't need a guy to be an Empowered Gal.* You don't even have to be all that into them, either. In fact, I hardly dated in high school because I didn't feel I had anything in common with guys my age. I had fun and went on some dates, but that was always the beginning and the end of it. I didn't feel I needed a guy to validate me. We gals are strong, sexy, capable women who don't *need* a man. The 1940s and '50s are in the past; the sexual revolution was forty years ago, and the idea that we need a guy to get by is about as outdated as poodle skirts and beehives!

This is the first time in history that single gals outnumber the married ones. I think that's kind of cool, actually. More women than ever are buying apartments, condos, and entire houses on their own. They're becoming CEOs of Fortune 500 companies, and some of the most powerful people in the media, publishing, fashion, beauty, advertising, marketing, and small-business fields are women. We women are taking exotic vacations, choosing our own paths, and deciding who and when—and if—we are going to have a partner to share it all with. So, if you are stressing out about being a single gal—don't! It's totally normal and totally fine, and there are about sixty good years ahead of you to date all you want!

With that said, dating *is* a big, fun, and exciting part of being a girl! Who doesn't love crushing on cute, funny, and nice guys, flirting, getting asked out (or doing the asking!), getting dressed up, and having a blast on a date? But remember, upon entering the dating world, you are going to be faced with drama, competition, and some mega-hurt feelings from time to time. But as long as you have realistic expectations, date for the right reasons, and go at your own pace, you'll be fine! Before you delve into the wonderful world of dating, let's check another IQ. You know the drill—just answer the following questions with a 1, 2, or 3.

What's Your Dating IQ?

1 = No way; 2 = Sorta, sometimes; 3 = Sure do!

1) I date based on personality, instead of status.	1	2	3
2) The guys I go out with or like are usually good guys.	1	2	3
3) I listen to my instincts when choosing guys.	1	2	3
4) I know I don't have to date anybody to feel good.	1	2	3
5) I know just 'cause my friends date doesn't mean I have to.	1	2	3
6) I don't center my life on guys.	1	2	3
7) I won't make him a priority if he won't make me one.	1	2	3
8) I handle breakups maturely and responsibly.	1	2	3
9) I know when enough is enough.	1	2	3
10) I know the qualities I want and don't want in a guy.	1	2	3

Now add up the numbers and find your Dating Gal IQ.   **Total:** _____

Scoring:

10-15: If your score is in this range, you're probably not into dating just yet, or you have no clue how to start—no worries. You have a ton of time ahead of you to date, so you don't have to start now. In fact, it's probably a good idea for you to stay single for a little while longer (or until you are totally ready), get to know yourself better, and date or don't date on your own terms. But whether you are ready or not, read on to discover the pros of being a single gal, and figure out what to expect when you *do* start dating.

16-22: If you're hanging in this middle of the road, you might be kind of interested in dating but not really ready to pursue it, which is totally cool. Or maybe you are just confused about the whole thing (join the club!). Either way, it's a good idea to have as much info as possible before you make any decisions, so pay extra attention to the dating smart section.

23-30: If you scored in this range, it looks like you have your PhD in dating-ology. Still, it never hurts to get a tip or two.

In "To Date or Not to Date," I'll discuss the pros and cons of dating in high school and help you figure out if you are ready to date—and why being a single gal is awesome, too. In "Dating Smart," I'll cover pretty much all there is to know about dating, from building a "guy sundae" to crushing smart and making the first move. Then, I'll go over everything you need to know to survive the first date, land a second, get what you want out the relationship, stay you-centered, and keep the relationship going strong. Oh, and you'll also learn fifteen super-fun, cheap date ideas, too! In "Breakups," I'll cover how you can decide when and how to end a relationship, coping with the aftermath, and figuring out if you should stay friends afterward.

Note: Not into guys but are digging girls instead? No prob. Just substitute "gal" for "guy" from here on out. Some stuff might not fit, but for the most part, dating is dating, and you'll still face a lot—if not more—of the pressure that goes along with it. And remember, whatever your preference, own it and rock it! There are tons of awesome lesbians and bisexuals out there for you to look up to, including Ellen DeGeneres, Melissa Etheridge, and Portia De Rossi.

To Date or Not to Date?

"I started 'dating' in kindergarten. I had a boyfriend constantly through high school and felt like I needed a guy to define me. I didn't know who I was without one. My last boyfriend and I broke up when I went to college. and I've been single ever since. It's been really hard. but I feel like I actually know who I am and can stand on my own. Now. when I get a boyfriend. I know I'll stand up for myself way more and pick a guy who is [right for] me."
—Jenna, 19

"Dating is really hard in high school. I don't have much in common with the guys in my school. and my parents don't want me dating college guys. so I'm still single and looking!"
—Devon, 17

"I'm going away to college next year. so I don't want to get too serious with my boyfriend. It's hard on him. but I have to do what's right for me."
—Allie, 17

"I have never dated anybody. My parents are pretty strict. and I have pretty conservative morals. and I worry that I might give in to temptation if I date anyone!"
—Sophie, 15

Most of us girls have the idea that we are better off in a relationship than—gasp!—being single. That seems to be the overall message we get from TV and movies. But the truth is, sometimes we are better off being on our own, and that's totally okay. You have to be happy being solo before you can be happy in a relationship, because dating doesn't make all your problems go away. If you are dealing with low self-esteem and have some mega-body issues, getting involved with a guy will probably only make them a whole lot worse. So, the first consideration when it comes to deciding whether or not you are ready to start dating is not based on what your friends are doing but how you are feeling.

Being in a relationship has the potential to disconnect you from yourself if you aren't fully grounded in who you are—and no matter who you are, that doesn't fully happen until your mid-twenties. So dating is fun and great, but it's important to consciously get to know yourself, nurture yourself, and set boundaries for yourself. It's okay to stay single until you feel ready to date, are happy on your own, and are ready to share yourself with somebody else. If you are still unsure, here are some signs that you may be ready to start dating:

- You are happy on your own and feel good about yourself.
- You respect yourself and your body.
- You feel ready to share your awesome self with somebody else.
- You know what qualities you are looking for in a partner.
- You can handle the drama that goes along with it. (Hint: It's a whole lot!)
- You have realistic expectations.
- You have supportive friends who will be there for you if it falls apart.

And remember, saying yes to the first guy who asks you out or shows any interest in you, just to avoid being alone, is not a good reason to start dating. Chances are, you both are going to be unsatisfied and disappointed, and to me, that sounds a whole lot worse than being a solo gal a little longer. You have your whole life ahead of you to meet people, date, flirt, and have a physical and emotional relationship with somebody, so don't worry. It's not like high school is your only time to date. And, if you feel like I did in high school—that you are the very last person on earth your age who hasn't gone on a date or had her first kiss—kick that crazy idea to the curb! You are not the last person; you are just among the lucky ones who have avoided a ton of heartbreak, disappointment, and drama up until this point!

There are some really great things about being in a relationship and really great things about being single. See what sounds best for you right now.

Great Things about Being Single

- You have more time to spend on things like friends, homework, and yourself.
- You can have as many crushes to daydream about as you want!
- You don't have to deal with all the drama that goes with dating.
- You don't have to choose between your friend or your guy.
- You can do what you want, when you want to do it!

Great Things about Being in a Relationship

- You get to find out another part of you—the coupled you.
- Getting to share everything with another person is pretty cool.
- You get a secure feeling of knowing you always have somebody on your team.
- You can do all the fun things couples can do!

Whatever you decide to do, it's totally up to you, and you should be proud of your decision. Do what feels right for you. Even if you've had a boyfriend since you were too young to walk, it's okay to take a break and get to know yourself before you commit to another guy (you little dating bandit!).

"The hardest situation to stay happy in. I think. is when you're trying to find love and yourself at the same time. It just doesn't seem to fit well."
—Sophia Bush, actress

Dating Smart

Dating smart is all about being responsible, respecting yourself, dating for the right reasons, loving yourself more, not being centered on the relationship, living up to your personal standards, being selective, and trusting your instincts. Dating *not* so smart is dating based on popularity, being pressured to date people you aren't all that into (just to be popular), rushing into things, being totally, BF-centered, dating every guy who shows the slightest interest in you, and ignoring your instincts.

Common Dating Myths—Busted

Having realistic expectations is a must when it comes to dating. Chick flicks and TV shows are awesome and all, but they kind of send the wrong message. And I'm pretty sure that's why guys would rather eat their own eyeballs than watch them with you—it's impossible for them to live up to the stuff in those movies. I mean, hello—how often do people actually:

- Have you at "hello"? (*Jerry Maguire*)
- Get married in the eleventh grade, split up, get back together, then have a kid together? (*One Tree Hill*)
- Fall in love with the mysterious boy online, who just turns out to be the school hottie? (*A Cinderella Story*)
- Get made over into a glamour girl as a prank, yet end up head over heels with the boy responsible for it? (*She's All That*)

I could go on! Instead, here are some common dating myths we are going to bust. (You're welcome, boys!)

Myth 1: It's gonna be like in the movies. No, it isn't. If you are expecting to fall in love with your first crush and get married, or even meet your dream partner in high school, you are going to be disappointed. Instead, expect to date several different people, if any at all, and be prepared to have your heart broken at least once before you find your Prince Charming.

Myth 2: Having a boyfriend = total happiness. Nope. It equals lots of great stuff if you are ready and with a good guy, but there are going to be ups and downs, fights, jealousy, confusion, and hurt feelings, and all the drama you had in your life before the boyfriend will still be there.

Myth 3: Looks matter most. All the sweet, nice, non-movie-star guys are going to be so happy we busted this myth! Looks obviously *do* matter, because they are what initially attract us to somebody, but without the goods (that is, the inner stuff), none of that Greek god stuff will matter. Things like personality, morals, and values are what will keep you interested in that person, so give the nice, cute, quirky guys a chance, ladies!

Know What You Want (What You Really, Really Want)

Just as there are many parts that make up a perfect ice-cream sundae, there are many parts that make up the "perfect" guy. The base, or the main parts, could be a scoop of chocolate (sense of humor), strawberry (kind and understanding), and Oreo cookie (smart and goal oriented). Then on top of that, once you have a good foundation of what matters most to you, you can start adding more personal preferences. Maybe you like hot fudge (dark and handsome) or possibly caramel drizzle (blonde, sweet, and beachy), and on top of that, just for fun, maybe you'd toss on some salted peanuts (daring, go-getter type) and some sprinkles (great personal hygiene), and the cherry on top could be that he loves his mom or is really romantic.

Use the following lists and space provided to figure out what your perfect guy (or sundae) looks like!

Ice Cream/Base:
- Vanilla = Trustworthy/honest
- Pralines and Cream = Hard working
- Chocolate = Sense of humor
- Strawberry = Kind and understanding
- Mint Chocolate Chip = Supportive
- Strawberry Cheesecake = Respectful
- Oreo Cookie = Smart
- Other:_____

Toppings:
- Chocolate Fudge = Tall, dark, and handsome
- Caramel Sauce = Blonde surfer dude
- Fruit = Preppy
- Sprinkles = Great hygiene
- Chocolate Chips = Athletic, fit
- Nuts = Daring, adventurous
- Candy = Good listener
- Whipping Cream = Energetic
- Other:_____

And the cherry on top = _____

_____

_____.

Bet you'll never look at ice cream the same way again! Did you notice the qualities that jumped out at you—those things that really mattered the most, and the stuff that would be great but not completely necessary for a delicious sundae? It's all about preference and giving new things a try, too. Maybe you don't usually like, say, gummy bears (quiet and shy), but if the yummy base is there, you might want to keep an open mind and give him … err, gummy bears … a chance.

"Some people are settling down, some people are settling, and some people refuse to settle for anything less than butterflies."

—Sarah Jessica Parker as "Carrie," on *Sex and the City*

Trust Your Instincts

The awesome thing about being a girl is that we come equipped with that all powerful intuition. Trust the feelings you get about people—your instinct to stay away from them or run into their arms—and listen to your gut when you have a bad feeling about somebody or something. We are taught to ignore that feeling because we can't see it or touch it, and there is no scientific data to prove it even exists.

I've always had really strong intuition. My great-grandmother was super-intuitive (she was a gypsy, and people still talk about all the things she knew), so I grew up in a household where that kind of thing was pretty normal. I learned to trust my feelings about things that would happen or people I would meet.

You should, too. If you get a feeling that a guy you meet at a party is no good, even though you have no "real reason" to think so, trust your instinct. Or, if you are on a date with somebody, and you get a really bad feeling about him, arrange for somebody to come to get you and take you home. Sure, you might look like a bitch, but I'd rather look like a bitch than wait around to be proven right about that bad feeling.

"Smile. Even when your life is at its worst, you never know when you'll meet the one who takes your breath away."
—Jessica Biel, actress

Have Self-Respect

If you don't treat yourself with respect, you can't fairly expect anybody else to do so. If you truly respect your body and your mind, you will naturally be drawn to people who do them same for themselves *and* for you.

- Be true to yourself.
- Act as smart as you are.
- Take time for you.
- Treat yourself to stuff you love to do, just for you.
- Stand up for yourself, and don't compromise your morals, values, or beliefs for anybody.
- Know you deserve the best, and don't settle for less than that.

Don't Be a Stupid Girl

The Jessicas and Parises of this world have used the "dumb blonde" approach to make millions of dollars. Personally, you couldn't pay me enough to act stupid. It is doing a disservice to ourselves and the guys we are hoping to attract. The truth is, there is only *one* thing a guy wants from girls like that. (Who wants to bring a ditzy girl home to meet Mom and Dad?)

Girls who know what they want, who are in charge of their lives, have it all together, and who are empowered to make their own decisions will intimidate most guys. The whole package freaks guys out. But by dumbing yourself down, you are showing them how to treat you—as dumb as you are acting. They will not respect you or take you seriously. It sounds harsh, but it is the truth, and you are better than that. And besides, why would you want to be with a guy who can't handle how empowered and smart you really are? You deserve a dude who will be knocked out by your beauty *and* your brains—and will treat you accordingly. The guys who like the stupid girls aren't worth your time.

Crushing

Crushing is fun, but you have to remember, it's called a "crush" for a reason! If he's "crushing" on another girl (not you), if he doesn't even know you exist, or if he is somebody you shouldn't be dating at all (maybe he's way older or unavailable), you are going to know all too well what getting crushed is all about. But with that in mind, you can still wallow in the unrequited love, daydream about your wedding day, and scribble your first name with his last name all over your loose-leaf paper. Here are the do's and don'ts of smart crushing:

Do become an expert small-talker. If you bump into him in line or corner him in the classroom, it's a good idea to have some stuff prepared, like:

- "Some test earlier, huh? Could you see the giant, glowing question mark above my head, or was that just me?" (Humor puts people at ease, so use it!)
- "Did you hear about (such and such)?"
- "Hey, I heard you made the team—congrats!"

Don't get stalker-ish. You don't need to hide out in the bushes outside his house, walk by his locker a thousand times a day, or dedicate a shrine in your room to him. Love from afar, sure, but make sure you aren't getting too obsessed.

Do make an effort. It can be scary, but try putting yourself out there in situations where you'll get to be around him, and try to get to know each other better.

Don't freak out if you embarrass yourself; it happens to the best of us. Laugh it off and move on. Dwelling about it won't change anything. If he can't joke around with you, he's probably not that crush-worthy anyway.

Do prepare yourself for the possibility he might not dig you back. It's not the end of the world; there are plenty of other crushable boys out there.

How to Tell If He Likes You Back

Now, this isn't as hard as in elementary school. (Hello? Is a punch in the arm really supposed to mean he likes you?) In high school, it gets a little easier. The guys are a little more mature, and you probably have a better understanding of them now. So, why does it seem so difficult to really tell if he likes you?

First of all, guys have these things called "Egos" (capitalized for a reason—they can sometimes be really big!). They don't want to look stupid, and they certainly don't want to be rejected, so they can send mixed signals. For example, when it's just the two of you, he may seem really into you, but when he's with his buddies, he may seem a little uninterested, leaving you super-confused.

It's always good to get to know this guy a little better. Once you know more about him, you'll be better able to decipher his "guy code." Here are some signs that he's definitely liking you back:

- He makes special effort to be with you, sit next to you, or hang out with you.

- He helps you with your homework, carries your books, etc.

- He stands up for and supports you.

- He compliments you on your clothes or hair or other little things.

- He has that goofy but super-cute smile on his face when he's around you.

- He "accidentally" bumps into you in the hallway.

- He takes the long way to his next class just to scope you out at your locker.

• He doesn't mention other girls in front of you, unless he's saying how much funnier, smarter, or cuter you are than they are.

Now, here are signs that he's not as into you as you hoped:
• He doesn't try spending time with you.

• He comments on other girls in front of you.

• He is more into his buddies—or other girls—than he's into you.

• He flirts with other girls just as much as he does with you.

• He's in an on-again/off-again relationship with another girl.

• He's a player.

The First Move: Who Makes it, When, Where and How?

If you really think he likes you back, there may be a couple reasons he hasn't made the first move, going back to the earlier mentioned ego. He could be unsure about how you feel about him and doesn't want to risk an ego-killing rejection if he asked you out and you said no. Or he could just be really shy. He could even be afraid of ruining a good friendship with you. You may never actually know the reason, but the good news is, this is the twenty-first century, and we gals can take matters into our own hands.

Taking Initiative—the Not So Scary Way!

First, start by dropping hints, hanging out with him, and getting to know him. Touch him on the arm or shoulder when you are talking to him, and show him that you like him, too. If this still doesn't get his attention, try saying something like this: *"I've really enjoyed the time we've spent together the past couple of weeks. It makes me wonder what it would be like to get to know you better and see where this can go."* You are still keeping it totally open, and you'll know for sure how he feels by his response. If he agrees, then maybe suggest going to dinner Friday night or whatever. If he makes a joke or seems uncomfortable, maybe he's not crushing quite as hard as you. Sure, that sucks, but give it time or move on. There are plenty of other guys out there who would love your love and affection and would be so super-lucky to be with you.

Here are some other "starter tips" for taking charge in the dating game and meeting new people:

- Join a club, start a hobby, or hang out with new groups of friends.
- Broaden your horizons. If you have been in love with the same boy since third grade and he doesn't seem all that into you, move on. Get to know new guys, and be open to hanging out with them.
- Ask your friends to set you up (on a double or group date) with a guy they know. You never know, right?
- Ask your crush out. It takes guts, but it beats sitting at home Friday night, waiting for a call if you really, really want to hang out with him!

Understanding Rejection

Nothing hurts quite as much as putting yourself out there and getting rejected. You instantly start making a mental check list of all the things that must be wrong with you. After all, it must be your fault, right? *Wrong!* Here's the thing: I hate mushrooms. I can't stand them. I think they are one of the grossest things on the planet. But lots of people *do* like mushrooms. In fact, some people even love mushrooms. So, there is nothing actually *wrong* with mushrooms; I just don't happen to like them, which is fine, because there are plenty of other people who would love to eat them. See what I'm saying? There is nothing wrong with you; it's just that different people have different tastes. You may not be right for him, but you are right for somebody else. Give yourself a break. (And I'll try to go a little easier on mushrooms.)

The First Date

Whether it's your first date *ever* or your first date with a particular guy, here are some things to remember to keep it running smoothly and have him begging for date number two!

- Generally, it's nice for guys to pay on the first date, but I think, as a rule, that the person who does the asking should pay. It's also fine to split the bill, so make sure you have some cash with you.
- Dress to impress *yourself.* He's dating you for you, right? Be yourself and wear stuff you feel super-pretty and comfortable in, not stuff you think would impress him, like by showing a lot of skin.
- Long periods of silence can be awkward before you get to know somebody, so before you go out, think of a couple questions to

ask him that require more than a simple yes or no answer, like, *"What did you think of last night's game?"* or *"How did you feel after you found out you got accepted at _____?"*

- Flirt, but just a bit. You don't want to seem over the top—that might cause him to run for the hills.

- Laugh, and be low key. If stuff doesn't go as planned, don't worry. The main point is that you two are together, so make the most of it.

- Have fun! It's not a trial marriage; it's a date!

- Whether or not you kiss on a first date is up to you, and it depends on lotsa stuff. But again, as a rule, I think a simple kiss on the cheek is good for a first date.

- Pick something fun to do. (Check out the list of 15 Cheap Date Ideas at the end of the section.)

Getting What You Want Out of the Relationship

A relationship should benefit both you and your boyfriend in a win/win sort of way. It should leave you both feeling satisfied, safe, respected, and free to be yourselves. Here are some things to check to see if your needs are being met.

- Do you feel safe, supported, and completely yourself when you are together?
- Is he there for you? Can you count on him? Is he meeting your emotional and physical needs?
- Do you trust him completely?
- Does he stick up for you and appear to always be on your side?
- Is he respectful of your boundaries and what is important to you?
- Does he make you feel good?
- Do you "fight fair" or is it always one-sided?
- When he says he's going to be someplace or do something, does he do it?

A good guy:

- Makes you laugh
- Makes you feel great about yourself
- Wants to know all about you

- Treats women like gold
- Loves his mama
- Doesn't treat you differently around different people
- Takes care of himself
- Gets good grades
- Has a good work ethic
- Doesn't drink or do drugs
- Doesn't make gross jokes that embarrass you
- Actually looks in your eyes when you talk
- Offers to do stuff for you
- Worships the ground you walk on—in a healthy kind of way, of course!

A bad guy:

- Makes you cry
- Talks only about himself
- Treats women like objects
- Drinks and does drugs
- Is failing his classes
- Doesn't work hard
- Doesn't believe in personal hygiene
- Has been with a *ton* of other girls before you
- Is a player
- Drains all of your energy
- Is hot and cold and all over the place with how he feels about you
- Plays games
- Calls you Kelly even though your name is Samantha.

"True love doesn't come to you; it has to be inside you."
—Julia Roberts, actress

Keeping a Relationship Strong

With all the drama associated with dating, it can be hard to keep a relationship running smoothly, but it can be done!

- Have time apart. He's not looking for a cling-on; he's looking for a girlfriend! And you can't miss somebody if he is always there.
- Be clear with your expectations.
- Have at least one night a week that is "date night," where you make time to do something special, just the two of you. (Hint: Pick a new date from the 15 Cheap Date Ideas coming up!)

- Do something sweet for each other, every day.
- Be respectful of each other's boundaries.
- Make sure you still have stuff in common, and you both want the relationship to work.
- Communicate. For a healthy, fulfilling relationship, communication is key. But a lot of guys would rather run head on into a cactus than talk about their "feelings." Be open about your feelings and expectations, and ask him to do the same.

"To be brave is to love someone unconditionally, without expecting anything in return. To just give. That takes courage, because we don't want to fall on our faces or leave ourselves open to hurt."
—Madonna, singer, actress

Balancing Friends with the Boyfriend and Staying You-Centered

Whether or not you are in a relationship, you should feel confident, fulfilled, and great about yourself all the time. If you go into a relationship looking for somebody to provide you with those things, you are going to get lost and forget that you are numero uno. A guy will seem more important to you, because you are relying on him for confidence and self-esteem, instead of supplying them for yourself.

You should never *need* a man. Want him, love him, adore him, and be with him, but don't ever *need* him for anything. If you begin to rely on someone else for your happiness, for the quality of your life, or for the things you want out of life, the best thing you can do for yourself is take a break, find yourself, discover what you are looking for on your own, and then give it another shot.

I look at my relationship as the icing on an already awesome, delicious cake. The cake would still be great without the icing, but that makes it just a little bit better. The mistake I made in the beginning of my relationship was that I thought my guy was the cake, and everything else was the icing. But what happens when there is no cake? The icing is just a pile of sugary mess on a cake stand, right? That's not what I wanted my life to be without him. I became responsible for making the cake the best it could be. I followed my dream, created my life the way I wanted it, felt great about myself on my own terms, and then shared it with him.

And don't forget about your pals! Your paired friends will be super-happy that you have a man of your own—double dates, anyone?—but your single friends may be less than stoked. It's important to hold on to your old life and who you are outside of the relationship. It's really easy to get caught up in him and wrap your world around him. But if your happiness and identity is held in one person's hands, it can have a disastrous effect on you and the relationship.

Don't be afraid to say no to doing stuff with your guy once in a while, and hang with friends or have solo time instead. It'll keep your identity going strong and independent from him, and it'll give you two the space you need to maintain a healthy relationship. Plus, you don't want to alienate the very people you might need to get you through a breakup, if that's what happens in the end.

Staying Safe: Avoiding Date Rape

I know this is a girl's worst nightmare, and for lots of us, it can become a reality. Date rape occurs when someone you know forces you to have sex with him, regardless of whether you are dating or have already had sex. It is never your fault, and it's nothing to be ashamed of. Here are some ways you can protect yourself:

- Don't drink alcohol—it can dull your senses, and if *he's* drinking, it can bring out aggressive or violent behavior.

- Watch your drinks. Drugs like GHB, "Roofies," or Ketamine can be mixed into your drink without your realizing it. Such drugs are usually colorless, odorless, and tasteless. They can make you black out or feel paralyzed and erase your memory of whatever went on.

- Avoid being alone with your date (even in your room, his room, or a vehicle) until you trust him, know him well, and feel comfortable with him.

- If you get a bad, uneasy feeling, follow your intuition and don't be alone with that person.

- If you go to a party, go with friends, and watch out for each other.

- Don't be afraid to yell, scream, or seem "rude" if you feel threatened. Your safety is the most important thing.

- Learn to protect yourself. Take self-defense classes to learn how to fend off an attacker.

No matter how safe and smart you are, date rape can still happen.

If it does, here's what you do:

- Go straight to the emergency room. It's a naturally tendency to want to wash him off you, but you'll be washing away valuable DNA evidence that could put your attacker behind bars. Plus, there will be counselors there to help you.
- Call your parents, friends, or somebody else you love and trust to be there with you.
- Find a quiet place and write down every single detail you remember.
- Surround yourself with supportive, understanding people. It might also be helpful to get counseling.

If you date smart and stay safe, dating in high school can be great—and fun, too! Check out these awesome date ideas!

15 Cheap Date Ideas (They are fun, too!)

1. Go to a school, church, or youth-group event together.
2. Search online for recipes, and challenge each other to make the best one!
3. Spend a Saturday afternoon at your house or his, watching a marathon of old movies, scary movies, or action movies, with bottomless popcorn and snacks.
4. Get your other coupled pals involved and have different competitions. Like, seeing who can raise more money for a charity, put together the craziest outfits from the thrift store, or divide into teams and make crazy movies or slide shows.
5. Volunteer at an animal shelter, walking dogs and playing with puppies and kittens.
6. Spend an hour at your local bookstore picking a book for each other, funny or serious. Then, grab an ice cream and head to a local park and exchange books. Or, go to the bookstore, find a nook, grab one of those books of questions that I mentioned earlier, and take turns asking and answering.
7. Do something physical—hiking, tennis, mini-golf, or Rollerblading.
8. Pack a picnic basket together, complete with yummy finger foods like fruit, mini-bagel sandwiches, bite-sized veggies and dip, and some sparkling lemonade. Don't forget the blanket and iPod with speakers to set the mood.
9. Go to a local fair, carnival, or playground and have fun!

10. Drive somewhere cool and watch the sunset, followed by a long walk and then a home-cooked meal.

11. Instead of spending all night at your friend's party, skip out early, grab a couple blankets, and do some star-gazing. Points go to whoever finds the Big Dipper first.

12. Spend a day together or with friends at a park, lake, or the beach. Light a fire (where permitted), and roast hot dogs and marshmallows.

13. Throw a party for the two of you and your other couple friends. Have everybody bring snacks and hang out around the pool, BBQ area, big screen, or karaoke machine.

14. Get to know each other by looking through old family photo albums.

15. Try something you've never done before, like snorkeling, skiing, go-cart racing, or water skiing.

Do these ideas sound fun, or do they sound fun?

But what happens when a relationship starts to fall apart? Read on for everything you need to know to survive a trip to Splitsville.

Breakups 101

"When I was 14. I thought I'd found my dream guy. but instead. he turned out to be a total nightmare! It was really hard and pretty scary at times. and [breaking up with him] was one of the hardest things I ever did. but I realize I deserved better."
—Danielle, 16

"It's always sad when a relationship starts to die. but there is no point in going down with the ship!"
—Catherine, 19

I'm just going to say it—breakups suck. You land your dream guy, things seem to be going great, and then "it" happens. It could be any number of things, but whatever "it" is, it's a sure sign you need to get outta there!

"It" #1: You grow apart. Totally normal thing to happen, especially if you have been dating for a while. It's natural for you two to change as you get older and get more life experience, but as you grow up, you may also grow apart. If you are starting to have different goals, ideas, motivations, and want or need different things, it might be best to end the relationship now, on friendly terms.

"It" #2: Controlling behavior. It may start out small, and you might even think it's sweet that he's "protective" of you. But being with a controlling partner is never sweet. If he calls you all the time to find out where you are; if you have to check in with him every hour; if he tells you what you can and can't wear, where you can and can't go, and who you can and can't hang out with, you need to get out of there fast! He might tell you that if you leave, he'll hurt you or himself. Or he might say that nobody else will love you like he does. Don't believe it; it's just part of his sick game. Don't be afraid to get help if you need to.

"It" #3: Abuse. Whether it's physical, emotional, or verbal, abuse is never okay, justified, or deserved. The abuser will make you feel like it's your fault, like you deserve it. He may tell you that nobody will believe you if you complain, or that he is doing it for your own good or because he loves you. If you are being abused, tell somebody you trust and get out of the relationship. I know it is hard, especially if he says he's sorry and that it will never happen again, that he didn't mean it, and that he loves you. But as far as I'm concerned, if a man ever abused me—particularly physical abuse—he'd only do it once. Hits and slaps are the tip of the iceberg. What follows is often beating, rape, being cut off from all your friends, made to feel worthless, and isolation from family—and it could end even more tragically.

Bottom line? Decide now what is and isn't acceptable, develop your self-worth, and know the difference between love and control. Then, you'll be so much better off if you ever encounter a weak, worthless, pathetic abuser.

"It" #4: Ultimatums. "If you don't have sex with me, I'll leave you" or "I'm not going to be with you if you don't start spending more time with me." These are examples of ultimatums–and they are never deserved. Being pressured into something is a sure sign that something isn't right. Before you cave to an ultimatum, be the one to break off the relationship.

How to Break Up

If you know the relationship isn't working for you and it needs to end, you have a responsibility to do so before it goes any farther. Otherwise, you both stand a greater chance of being hurt. It's up to you to handle it in a classy, adult way—not like I did in eighth grade, when I had about four girls corner the poor boy and do it for me. (Steve, if you are reading this, I am sorry!) Or like I did a year later, when I just kind of didn't tell him at all. Or like I did the year after that, when I told the poor guy in the hallway outside of math class with everybody walking by. Or like I did a year after *that*, when I left for England for three weeks without saying anything. Yeah, not so stellar a track record.

But I know now what *not* to do, so here's what I've learned. It's hard to be on either end of a breakup, but the person who's being told it's over is going to feel a little worse. Break up in a way that shows you care for and respect him. And remember:

- Find a quiet place without a million people zooming by to break the news to him.
- Do it in person. We all remember the Post-it note that Burger used to dump Carrie in *Sex and the City*, and that, my friend, is just not cool.
- If your split occurs mid-fight, it may or may not be all over. If you want it to be official, make it so when you both have calmed down, or talk it out to make sure you didn't just make a snap decision in the heat of the moment.
- Be kind if he's totally in love with you, and let him down easy.

- If you are super-mad at him for something, it's okay to let him know what he did was *so* not okay with you, and you aren't going to tolerate it.
- Tell him how you feel, and tell him that you'd appreciate it if you could both keep it friendly.

Saying something like this usually works: "Hey, David, we need to talk. *(That tips him off that something serious is coming, so he can prepare.)* You may have noticed the past couple of weeks that things were a little weird. The truth is, as much as I love and respect you as a friend, this whole relationship thing just isn't working. I've got a lot on the go, and I know you do to, so let's try to cool this off."

Insert your own stuff and reasons in there, but that should give you a good start. Just don't accuse, blame, or get mad at the poor guy. He's just lost his dream girl, so be kind!

But what if you are the one *getting* dumped? Whether or not you expect it, it can be hard and a major blow to the ego. Just remember the mushroom analogy from earlier—maybe you're just not his flavor. As tough as it is, try not to beg, grovel, or grab hold of his leg and refuse to let go until he reconsiders. Instead, stay classy, keep your composure, and take the high road. There is no need to name call, freak out, or take a Louisville slugger to both headlights, à la Carrie Underwood—although, admittedly, it would feel good. No one breakup is the same, so how you react depends on lots of things, like how long you have been dating, the reasons for the split, etc. Maybe you'll want to talk it out, stay friends, or break off all communication completely. Just as long as you don't fly his underwear from the flagpole, spread every personal tidbit about him around school, or plaster flyers with his face and a nasty comment all over town, I'd say whatever you do is just fine!

LAB: Life after the Breakup

I wish I were talking about a cute little puppy, but the LAB I'm talking about is Life After the Breakup. LAB can be awkward and confusing—and that's if all goes well. Nobody likes to bump into her ex in the hallway, especially in the week or weeks following the split. It hurts, even if you are the dumper, not the dumpee. So, what can you do to help you deal?

- Let yourself be bummed out. It's normal, so give yourself a couple days where you cry, watch sad movies, and draw devil horns on his pictures. A tub of Ben and Jerry's may or may not be needed, but get one anyway.

- Do "you" stuff. Once the initial sadness goes away, do stuff to help you reconnect to you, like going for a walk, reading a good book, or watching your favorite shows in a day-long marathon.
- Write it all out in a letter, being as detailed as you can about how you feel and what you want him to know. Then, immediately put it in an envelope and stick it directly into the fire. You will feel lots better!
- Hang out with your friends, flirt a little with other guys, and do stuff you didn't have time for when you were coupled.
- Do something to change it up a bit, like dye your hair, get fake nails, slap on a henna tattoo, get a new shade of lip gloss, or get an awesome new haircut to symbolize a "new you" or at least a new stage in your life.
- Move on by either deciding to stay single for a while, or keeping an eye out for a new crush. Hey, now you are one step closer to finding the right guy for you!

But then what? Should you stay friends with him or not? Here's what you need to know.

Stay friends if ...

- You were friends before, and you ended on good terms.
- He never abused you in any way.
- He is a really great guy, and he is somebody you truly care about.
- Your romantic feelings are over (and so are his).
- You are both mature enough to put the past behind you and create a new relationship.
- You won't be jealous of seeing him with other girls.

Don't stay friends if ...

- You met out of the blue, and ended on bad terms.
- He was unfaithful, lied, cheated, stole, or used you.
- The relationship was based on looks or what you could do for each other socially.
- You are jealous of his being with other girls.
- You still have romantic feelings for the guy (or vice versa).
- He abused you physically or emotionally.

If you really loved the guy, if he treated you with respect and never hurt you, and if things ended as well as could be expected, then working on a friendship with him can be a healthy and positive experience—

after you give yourself (and him) time to get over it and move on. It's nice to think that you could stay friends with every guy you dated, but that isn't always the case. After all, dating in high school is often based on things like social status, "hotness," peer pressure, and trying to make yourself feel loved, and that can lead you down the wrong path to the wrong guy.

Gal to Gal

"The best piece of advice I ever got was from my mom. She said the most important thing to do was just follow my heart. To go with it if it feels right. and as soon as my heart's not in it. either change it. or follow it somewhere else."
—Amanda, 18

"Just be yourself. It's never worth changing yourself for a guy. He either will like you for you. or he won't."
—Sudah, 17

"Know you are more than just a part of a relationship. Don't give up your dreams just because you think you found your dream guy."
—Taylor, 18

"It's important to be realistic and to also keep an open mind. You never know what might happen!"
—Mackenzie, 14

"I'd have to say the most important piece of advice for dating is just to do it for fun. As soon as you start getting bored. upset. controlled. or it's getting too serious or interfering with your friends. school. and family. move on."
—Jaz, 15

Hey, it's okay to:
- Not want to date yet or be super-excited about bagging yourself a boyfriend. Do what's right for you!
- *Like* two different types of sundaes at once; just don't *have* them both at once!
- Eat an entire pint of ice cream upon breaking up with your boyfriend. Sometimes, that's what is required!
- Want a crush to remain a crush, nothing more.

-Stay tuned for Sex-Smart Gal, where you will find out what he *really* means when he says what he says, how to deal, and a ton of tips and advice from somebody who has been there and isn't afraid to spill about the stuff you need to know and that your parents probably haven't told you. Turn the page, and I'll meet ya there.

Lesson 5:

Sex-Smart Gal 101

S-E-X. Yup, I said it. Now, if you have a pulse, you've thought about sex, one way or another. You are either totally into it (maybe you've already been there … done that!), or you are so grossed out by it that you threw up a little bit in your mouth just reading the word. Whatever your position on sex (the first of many puns), it's your bod, and it's up to you what you do with it. So, before you decide what to do, get the info you need to make the best decision for you, uncover some sex myths, and see why it's a good idea to wait.

"It's a woman's spirit and mood a man has to stimulate. ... The real lover is the man who can thrill you by touching your head or smiling into your eyes or just staring into space."
—Marilyn Monroe

Whether you've done it (loved it or regretted it), want to do it, are not going to do it until you are married, or are pretty undecided about the whole thing, you've made decisions along the way that have led you to where you are now. I hope those decisions were right for you and that you are happy with the results (or maybe you wish you could have a do-over). Whatever the case may be, the decisions you make from this point on are the ones that matter the most. You can start fresh, armed with all the info you'll ever need about making smart, informed decisions about sex that work for you.

And just so you know, this isn't one of those teen books where the author says "Don't have sex...EVER!" because she thinks that is what will make parents buy it. I'm saying it's up to you. The only right or wrong decision here is whether it is right or wrong for you. I believe that's all that matters, and I want you to be happy with the ones you make, now and in the future. But in order to know what choices to make, you need to be educated, self-aware, and mature enough to deal with the consequences (as well as the fun stuff), so take this snazzy little quiz to help you figure out your Sex-Smart IQ.

Just choose 1, 2, or 3.

Your Sex-Smart Gal IQ

1 = No way; **2** = Sorta, sometimes; **3** = Sure do!

1) I know about STDs and how they are transmitted.	1	2	3
2) I value and respect my body.	1	2	3
3) I know I am worth waiting for.	1	2	3
4) I know my morals and values and stick to them.	1	2	3
5) I feel comfortable talking to my 'rents about sex.	1	2	3
6) I use/would use protection every time.	1	2	3
7) My friends make good decisions about sex.	1	2	3
8) I am open when talking about sex with guys.	1	2	3
9) I feel loved and worthy without having sex.	1	2	3
10) I am prepared to deal with *all* the consequences of sex.	1	2	3

Now add up the numbers and find your Sexy Gal IQ.   **Total:** _____

Scoring:

10-15: If you scored somewhere in here, you are either way not into sex (*totally, totally fine!*) or you don't love, value, and respect yourself enough to even think about having it right now. Either way, it's a good idea to spend some more time getting to know yourself before you take the plunge. Remember, you have a lifetime ahead of you to have sex, so there is no real or imagined race to the finish line.

16-22: Maybe you are interested in sex but not ready for it, or maybe you *think* you are ready but are still kind of unsure. Or, maybe you've already had sex and regretted it or are being pressured into it as we speak. Either way, you owe it to yourself to educate yourself about all things sex, from the emotions involved and how you will feel after, to protecting yourself and finding out why waiting until you are ready is the best option.

23-30: Well, somebody paid attention in sex ed (or has read every *Cosmo* magazine printed!). But this is a whole different type of sex ed, so there are probably one or two things you need to know to stay safe, happy, and in control.

This is a touchy subject (again with the puns, I do apologize), but it is one of the most important areas to be empowered in. These decisions are big, adult, real-world decisions that girls seem to be making younger and younger. In "To Do It or Not to Do It," I'll cover everything you need to consider and be prepared for before you decide to have sex. I'll help you to understand what guys really mean when they say what they say, and why it's totally fine (and recommended) to wait until you are ready. "Doing the Deed: What You Need to Know" is for you girls who decide you are ready for sex (or are already having sex). It will let you in on what to expect, how to deal with your first time and the "after thoughts" you may experience, and how to take ownership of your sexuality in an empowered way.

To Do It or Not to Do It

"I had the best first time ever. It was with the same guy I'm with now, and it was amazing! We waited until we really loved each other, were comfortable with each other, and we took is really slow. We are getting married in the fall, and I couldn't be happier that I waited for the right guy."
—Shayla, 22

"I had sex when I was fourteen, and it really freaked me out. I didn't do it again until I was seventeen, and it was way better that time."
—Jose, 18

"I have had eight partners and I'm only seventeen. Sometimes I feel really bad about myself, and I wish I had waited a little longer, or at least not had so many partners."
—Ashanti, 17

"I'm waiting until I'm married before I have sex."
—Laura, 18

On one hand, you have your parents telling you to wait until you are thirty, desperately hoping the whole "cootie" thing is still very real in your mind. Your sex ed consists of "abstinence only" education, which, in case they haven't noticed, doesn't work because tons of teens are having sex without the vital info they need to protect themselves, mentally and physically. Then, your friends are encouraging you to "just do it already; it's no big deal." And let's not forget your boyfriend, who is practically leading the march for you to give it up. You have probably been made to feel like the very last person your age who is still a virgin, and you're doing whatever you can to cover up the neon "V" on your forehead. All your favorite TV characters have done it, are in the process of doing it, or are planning to do it in the next episode.

Yet it is all a huge contradiction in the end. If you do it, you're a slut; if you don't, you're a "tease." If you don't want to do it, there is something wrong with you. And if you do it with more than one person, you might as well just leave town completely.

And amid all that, you are trying to do what is right for you, which, by now, has gotten way tangled up in what everybody else wants you to do. Hello? Does it really need to be this hard? I think not. Let's back up for a minute.

Your choice to have sex (or not to have sex) and who you will have sex with are all super-personal choices that vary greatly from one girl to another. What works for your friends may or may not work for you. You have to take everything into consideration and understand where everybody is coming from.

Parents. They want what's best for you, believe it or not! They aren't out to ruin your life. They have been there, done that, and as much as you hate to hear it, they have way more experience with sex than you. They know what it's all about, how you feel afterward, and the impact it can have on your life. When they say "No, absolutely not, never," understand that they are really saying "I love you so much. Please wait—it's for your own good!"

Teachers. Teachers see thousands of kids walk though their doors. They've seen it all, including girls getting pregnant and leaving school. They probably know abstinence-only education doesn't work, but they want you to stay safe and be baby- and STD-free when you graduate high school.

Boyfriends. No hidden agenda there—they just want to get it on with you! You see, there are these sneaky little things called hormones, and boys have lots of them. But so do you. See the dilemma?
It can be confusing! That's why you have to remember, it's called sex-*u*-ality, not sex-*him*-ality, sex-*their*-ality or sex-*anybody-else*-ality. It's all about you, baby—your wants, needs, desires, feelings, and body. Sex should never happen unless you are both digging it; it's not about just him or just you. It's about both of you, and if either one of you isn't ready, that's fine. And remember, nobody ever regretted *waiting*. Some girls wait for marriage, love, or a certain age. Some wait until after they reach certain goals, like graduating, or some just wait for "when it feels right." Whatever you choose, it's totally awesome, and you should own it. It's *your* decision. And just so you know, when I say "sex," I mean any form of it, because it all counts, and it's all a big deal!

Bed-Hopping Bandits

I'm all about young women embracing their sexuality, but I think it should be done in an empowered way. Sleeping with random guys is not a celebration of empowerment. I've never heard of a girl who actually enjoyed sleeping with guys she barely knew. If you find yourself doing that, ask yourself what you are really looking for. Is it love? Comfort? Male attention? There are way better ways to go about getting those things, and they don't involve putting your mental and physical well-being at stake.

How do you feel after you give your body up to some guy you barely know? Or when you perform oral sex on some guy you just met? I can't imagine that "proud" jumps to mind. And I'm not trying to make you feel bad or tell you what to do. I just want you to value yourself a little bit more. Girls aren't blow-up dolls, ready for any guy to use whenever he wants. If you want respect, you have to respect yourself first.

Become a Sexpert

The decisions you make regarding sex are some of the most important decisions you will make in your teen years, because the consequences of making bad ones can last a lifetime. You need to know everything you can about sex. Get super-comfortable talking about it, and educate yourself on the risks involved, both physically and emotionally. Here are some steps you can take to make sure you are a sex expert:

- Go to www.scarleteen.com, one of *the* best places to go online for info on sex.

- Talk to your friends, parents, and girls who have been there before. Chances are, everybody will have had a different experience, and the more you talk about it, the more comfortable you get, and the better able you are to make the right decisions.

- Read books. There are a ton of great books on sex at your local library and bookstore, so check them out. I recommend *S.E.X.: The All-You-Need-to-Know Progressive Sexuality Guide to Get You Through High School and College* and *Deal with It! A Whole New Approach to Your Body, Brain, and Life as a gURL.*

Once you have all the facts, you'll be way better able to make the right decisions for *you.*

EG Tip: Have you had a first-time or previous sexual experiences you regret? Whether you were too young, pressured into it, or too drunk to really remember, it doesn't mean that the rest of your sexual future has to be the same. And just 'cause you've done it before doesn't mean that you need to keep doing it. Wait 'til you're ready, and make the next time count! And don't feel bad; we all make mistakes. Make a pact with yourself to honor yourself a little bit more, and move on!

No apologies.

It may seem that guys are getting a bad wrap here, but that's because they don't stand to be as hurt, confused, or upset as you do if something goes wrong. They don't have to live with being a teenage mother, putting their entire academic career on hold while they take care of a baby. They don't get pregnant—you do! I'm not as much *against* guys as I am completely and totally *for* gals! So, here is your ultimate guide to decoding guy lingo! (Sorry, guys, just sticking up for my gals here!)

"If you love me, you'll have sex with me." The decision to have sex has to be for you, not for anybody else, and it doesn't matter how many times you might have had it before. Love is more than just a fleeting feeling in a boy's pants; it is a connection with and a commitment to another human being. If a guy says that you need to sleep with him in order to prove your love for him, you know exactly what organ he's thinking with. (Hint: It's not his heart!)

The Empowered Gal's Answer: "If you love me, you'll stop pressuring me, and wait for me to be ready. This is a really big decision that isn't about showing you how much I love you. It's about me showing me how much I love *me*, and when I'm ready, I'll let you know."

"Stop being such a tease!" Who wants to be a tease? Nobody, right? So, when a guy tells you to stop being a tease, you immediately feel guilty for leading him on. That's what he wants you to think. But being guilted into having sex with somebody isn't a good reason to do it. If you crumble to this pressure, you are totally going to regret it later. He's a creep for even bringing guilt into the picture.

The Empowered Gal's Answer: "If you feel I am being a tease, you have gotten the wrong message. I am expressing the way I feel about you in a way that I am comfortable with. I am not willing to go any further than this right now. If and when the time is right, I'll let you know"

"Everybody else is doing it." Nope. Not true. Sure, more girls are having sex at a younger age now than, say, fifteen years ago, but by no means does that mean "everybody." In fact, according to the Centers for Disease Control and Prevention, only about 46.8 percent of girls in high school are having sex; it decreased 13 percent between 1991 and 2005. And who cares about "other people," anyway? You are not everyone else—you are you, and you need to do what's *right* for you.

The Empowered Gal Answer: "Everybody is *not* doing, and even if they *were*, I am still not ready, and I'm fine with that."

"What's wrong with you? Don't you want to make me happy?"
What teenage girl doesn't think there is something wrong with her? I did, when I was in high school, along with every other girl in my class! Combined with a lower-than-normal self-esteem, this comment can really strike a chord, because you think to yourself, "*Is* there really something wrong with me?" And who doesn't want to make somebody they care about happy? When a guy tells you this, though, you know he's got his game face on and is going in for the win. Gals, he just wants to score! But because you know his game, you won't fall for it.

The Empowered Gal's Answer: "Just because I'm not ready to have sex with you doesn't mean that there is something wrong with me. It's not about making *you* happy; it's about respecting myself and my body enough to wait until the time—and the guy—is right."

"You've done it before, so what's the big deal?" It's your body— that's the big deal! Just because you let your friend borrow your car doesn't mean you are going to let a stranger take it for a drive as well! Some guys think that just because you've had sex before (whether it was two or twenty-two times), then you are going to give it up for him, too. No way. You deserve more than that.

The Empowered Gal Answer: "Yeah, I have done it before. And just because I'm not a virgin anymore doesn't mean I'm fair game for everybody. It's a big deal to me, and I chose who I want to be with, and when I'm ready to be with him."

"I love you, and I want to show you how much I love you."
Ahh, that one gets girls every time. After all, who doesn't want to be loved, told they are beautiful, and be made to feel important and cared for? The only thing is ... does he really mean it? In high school, the first time I spoke to my boyfriend on the phone, he told me he loved me. Sweet, yes, but it wasn't love. His penis might have loved me, but *he* didn't. He may have been "in lust" with me, but he certainly didn't love me. As good as it may be to hear those three words, make sure he *shows* you he loves you *outside* of the bedroom. And make sure the first time he tells you isn't with a condom in his hand and a grin on his face.

The Empowered Gal's Answer: "It means a lot to me that you feel that way, but I'm just not there yet. I think you are great, and I really want to get to know you better." Or "I love you too. And if you really do love me, then please stop pressuring me, and wait for me to be ready."

"I'll break up with you if you don't sleep with me." If anybody pressures you to this extent to have sex with him, honey, he is not worth a second more of your precious time. Nobody deserves an ultimatum like this, no matter what. Whether you've been going out ten days or ten months, it's *so* not acceptable. As hard as it is, do yourself a favor, and move on. You deserve to be with somebody who respects your mind *and* your body—and your individual right to make choices for yourself.

> **The Empowered Gal Answer:** "Let me beat you to it. It's over. I deserve way better than you. If you feel that way, then I don't want to be with you, either."

EG Tip: "No" is a full sentence here, gals! You don't need to explain yourself or offer reasons or excuses. It's a powerful word, so own it!

Other Ways to Be Intimate

I totally get the appeal of wanting to be intimate with somebody. It's new, exciting, and looks like a lot of fun on TV, but there is a lifetime ahead of you, when you'll be mentally and physically ready to explore the physical side of a relationship. If you want to experience intimacy with somebody without sex, there are plenty of ways to do it:

- **Give a massage.** Instead of rounding second base, a great way to feel great and get comfortable with another person is to touch in nonsexual ways. For instance, take turns giving each other back and neck rubs. The trick here is to have clear expectations and boundaries going into it. No sexual contact, kissing, or nudity allowed—that will keep it really sweet and romantic, instead of super-sexual.
- **Cook a romantic dinner together.** Food can be super-sensual and romantic. Plan a menu, cook it together, and feed it to each other by hand. No forks allowed!
- **Making out/dry humping.** This is kind of like the final frontier before actual sex. It's like a warm-up round, but you are still safe from babies and diseases. It doesn't require much explaining, but you two must have boundaries before you start. I know, I know—*so* not sexy to talk about, but be clear with your expectations and what is and isn't allowed, and come up with a code word that means stop right now, thank you very much!

The Importance of Protection

Why is protection important? Well, if things like syphilis, scabies, pelvic inflammatory disease, pubic lice, or herpes don't sound like any fun for you, using a condom—every time—is a must. Still not convinced? Maybe these facts and stats will do the job.

- According to the Centers for Disease Control and Prevention (CDC), one-quarter of all teens will get a sexually transmitted disease (STD).
- Half of all new HIV infections occur in young people; 232 young people die of it each year, and in 2004 alone, 4,883 people, aged 14–25, were diagnosed with HIV, according to the CDC. It *can* happen to you.
- The Pill or other forms of hormonal birth control methods *do not* protect you from any STD, including HIV.
- You *can* contact an STD through unprotected oral sex.
- There are over twenty different kinds of STDs (and none of them are any fun).
- The Centers for Disease Control and Prevention estimates that half of teens who have sex will contract an STD by the time they are 25 (yes, that's *half*, ladies), and eight million young people between 14 and 25 are diagnosed with an STD each year.
- You *can* get pregnant your first time—many do.
- Condoms don't protect you 100 percent from all STDs; for example, HPV (the most common sexually transmitted infection) is spread through skin-to-skin contact in the areas *not* covered by a condom.

Ever heard of a game called Russian roulette? The true origin of the game isn't really known, but basically, a revolver was loaded with one, single round (bullet), and then soldiers, gamblers, or prisoners or war would take turns putting the gun to their heads and pulling the trigger. The game winner was the one left alive at the end. Crazy, right? So is having sex without protection. **You have a 25 percent chance of getting an STD within a year if you have unprotected sex—so don't play Russian roulette with your body.** The next time you are thinking of pulling a Juno, stop and ask yourself if the risk is really worth the reward.

You are responsible for your body, and you are gonna be in it for the rest of your life, so you better make sure you take care of it. No boy is worth putting yourself at risk. If he won't have sex without a condom, tell him that he has a left hand that is more than happy to have unprotected sex with him. If, on the other hand, he wants to have sex with a living, breathing woman, he might want to reconsider wearing protection.

You also need to consider who is going to be responsible for providing the protection. (Hint: It's your body; you and only you are responsible for protecting it. If you are sexually active, always keep condoms with you, and *use them*, even if you are on the Pill or using some other kind of hormonal method.)

The Secret Lives of STDs

STDs are scary, and they often lie dormant or have few or no symptoms. What does that mean? They can go undetected, and you can pass them onto other partners, who in turn, pass them onto other people. You are, in fact, having sex with every person your partner has had sex with, and all the people that *those people* have had sex with. And lotsa times, those silent STDs, like HPV, can lead to cervical cancer and infertility. See what I mean about big-time consequences later in life? Condoms are *non-negotiable*. If you don't love yourself enough to use them, you should wait to have sex until you do. But as scary, dangerous, and real as STDs are, they aren't the only possible (and likely) consequence of unprotected sex, especially if you aren't using a backup method.

OMG-BABIES!

Nothing freaks me out more than seeing a fourteen-year-old with a baby. Sure, you are obviously physically capable of creating one, but do you really want the responsibility of raising another human being when you are still a kid yourself? And let's not forget about how they actually come out. Yikes!

According to the National Campaign to Prevent Teen Pregnancy, three in ten girls will become pregnant in their teens, and that's a whole lot of babies who need to be loved, fed, nurtured, educated, bathed, played with, and whatever else it is you do with babies. Now, if you're like any other teen, you barely have time to shower, so how do you think you'll be able to raise another person?

I know there are some great young moms out there who have totally stepped up and gone the distance, but it's not easy. There are some major sacrifices you have to make, including not being able to:
• Party and hang out with your friends

- Possibly finish your high school or college education
- Go out on Friday nights
- Be selfish and think only about yourself
- Date freely
- Spend money on clothes, makeup, and entertainment

There are also lots of girls who *want* to get pregnant, even going to the extreme of poking holes in condoms. I don't really know where to start! First of all, there are plenty of other ways to feel loved or special that *don't* include giving birth. Second, it's kind of selfish to do that to the kid *and* the dude. And third, STDs, anyone?

I get that you might think that a baby will solve all your problems, but you'll still have the same old problems as before, just with a whole bunch of new ones. A baby is a miracle, and it will change your life, but for your own sake and the baby's, wait until you are a little older, are finished with your education, and can support yourself and your baby.

If you are one of the many young teens who have a baby or are preggers now, your life isn't over. Your old life is, but there is a whole new one ahead of you. You have to step up *now*—not two weeks from now or nine months from now. You are—or about to be—a mommy, so it's not just all about you anymore. Now, more than ever, you have to graduate, get a great job, and start taking care of the little one, Ask for help 'cause you'll need it, and work extra hard to make it. You can still reach all your goals and dreams, but it'll be a different journey to the destination.

Why Abstinence IS Awesome

Lots of teens are all about waiting—in fact, according to a recent study by *Seventeen* magazine, 52 percent of you plan on staying a virgin until your wedding night. If that's you, or you just want to wait until you are in love or have finished school, there are lots of benefits to waiting.

- Seventy-one percent of girls wish they would've waited, according to the CDC.
- You don't have to deal with any of the stressful stuff mentioned above, like STDs or pregnancy.
- You will be less stressed out and have more energy to put into your schoolwork, friends, and family.
- You can enjoy being a carefree (okay, mostly carefree) teen.
- There is no chance of a leaked sex tape to ruin your rep. (Hey, in this day and age, that's a major consideration!)

- The guys who stick around (when they know they absolutely are not going to "get lucky" with you) might just be keepers.

There you have it, ladies! Sex is a really big decision, so if you aren't ready, wait until you are.

This next section is for you gals who feel ready to give it a shot or are already sexually active.

Doing the Deed: What You Need to Know

You have weighed all the options. You respect yourself and your body. You are with a great guy and you haven't been pressured. And *you* want to and are ready to have real-life, honest-to-goodness sex. You are probably a little bit nervous. You don't know what to expect and maybe you'd like to go over everything one more time before you go for it, just to be sure. Okie dokie! Here are some things you need to know:

- It isn't going to be like movie sex.
- It may or may not make you closer to your guy; may or may not make the relationship stronger—there are no guarantees.
- It isn't going to be the most pleasurable (or most painful) experience of your life. It's different for everyone.
- It won't make you a "woman" or more grown up. You'll still be the same old you, just the non-virgin version.
- If you are doing it to keep a guy, make him happy, make a relationship stronger, impress your friends, or any other reason that doesn't involve your happiness and pleasure, stop right there. Sex won't do any of that, and you'll end up getting hurt—and that's a guarantee.

The Ultimate "Am I Ready?" Checklist

Still think you are ready? Let's double-check. If you can answer yes to all of the following points, then you might be ready to have sex, not before.

- I am comfortable talking about sex with my partner.
- I'm okay talking to a trusted adult about it.
- I can use the proper names for body parts without blushing.
- I have talked to my doc about protection against STDs and pregnancy, and the emotional effects of having sex.

114

- I am okay if the relationship changes, if we break up, or if the entire school finds out that we did it.
- I can afford the monthly expense of birth control and STD protection—usually around fifty dollars a month.
- I have a support system of friends and family to be there for me if I get dumped, labeled, pregnant, or get an STD.
- I love and value my body and am making a decision for me because I know I'm the one who has to live with the decision the rest of my life.
- My partner is loving, supportive, and understanding.
- I understand that I can change my mind and say no at any moment.
- I am in a committed relationship.
- I am educated about different STDs and their causes, symptoms, and treatment.
- I am able to deal with the physical, mental and financial side effects of pregnancy and STDs.
- I'm comfortable with kissing and touching.
- I am on a medical plan that will help with the costs if I get pregnant or contract an STD and need treatment.

Your First Time

I'm not gonna lie to you—sex is nothing like they make it out to be on TV or in the movies, and some people feel kind of disappointed when it doesn't live up to all the mega-hype that's out there. Your first time will probably be kind of awkward, maybe funny, slightly confusing, and a little exciting, but it's not so earth-shattering or life-changing an experience that you'll wake up the next day, ready to take on the world. Still, it can be a really great experience, especially if you choose the right guy, are 100 percent ready, and keep the following tips in mind:

- Talk about it in advance—how you feel, what you expect, etc.
- Choose a comfortable, safe place. No back alleys or seats of cars! If you like, light a couple candles, put on a Sade CD, and dim the lights to make it even more special.
- Take it really slow, and make sure you are comfortable with every step. You might want to keep a bottle of latex-safe lube next to the condoms to help things go a little more smoothly.
- Be realistic! He's probably just as nervous as you are, so don't worry if there are a couple screw-ups along the way.

- Enjoy it! You only get one "first time," so make sure it's worth remembering, 'cause you will never forget it. The more relaxed and sure you are, the better it is going to be *and* feel.
- Laugh! It relaxes you both, takes a ton of pressure off, and makes it way more fun. And let's be realistic—sex can be super-funny. If you make a weird noise, fall off the bed, or do something else cringe-worthy, laugh it off. There is no need to be embarrassed by anything that happens, and if the guy makes you feel bad about yourself, stop it right there, and wait for somebody who will make you feel comfortable.

After Thoughts

How you'll feel after sex depends on a lot of things, like your partner, your reasons for doing it, and your age. Studies show that the older you are when you have sex, the better it is and the fewer regrets you have. Sex isn't just physical—that's the easy part. You see, ladies, we have these things called emotions, and they can get seriously screwed up if we don't make the right decisions. I remember thinking that I would feel so different after having sex, like I'd wake up a new person. I didn't. It was amazing, but I was still the same old me. But I know girls who wake up the next day who *do* feel different. They feel used, dirty, or ashamed, because they were pressured into it, were drunk, or were just trying to impress somebody, none of which is a great reason to do it, whether it's your first or twenty-first time!

There is a good chance you are going to feel a lot of unfamiliar and perhaps unexpected emotions afterward, even if it is just disappointment. You may feel really emotionally attached to your boyfriend and even act a little clingy. You might be kind of depressed and bummed out because you are no longer a virgin and are confused about your new sexual identity, or you may be bouncing off the walls because you loved it so much.

Tori Spelling, who's sometimes been called "TV's most famous virgin," recently wrote about her first time and her "after thoughts" and feelings in her book *sTORI Telling*. She said that after, even though she was eighteen and thought she loved the guy, she went home, got into bed, and cried. She writes: "I'd shut the door on my childhood. If that doesn't deserve a good cry, I don't know what does." You might feel any number of different ways, and I can't tell you how you, personally, will feel. All I can do is suggest that you wait until you are ready—truly, madly, deeply ready—whatever that looks and feels like to you.

Making It Great—Every Time

So, you decided to have sex. Maybe it was what you expected, maybe it was something totally out of this world, but if you choose to keep having sex, here are some things you need to know to make it great—because it should be. Sex is a celebration of you, and it should make you feel good. Sometimes, though, your partner will need a little guidance, and you'll have to tell him (or her) what you like.

- Speak up. Totally not digging his little "technique"? You don't have to grit your teeth and bear it. Try letting him know that you prefer *this* move or like it better when he does *that*.
- Have boundaries. You will be way more comfortable if you have firmly established your boundaries first. If "a" and "b" are okay, but "c" totally freaks you out, tell him you aren't going there or doing that.
- Figure out what you like—on your own. There is no better way to figure out what works for you than a little "one on one." And contrary to popular belief, it's not going to make you go blind, and it's certainly not dirty or shameful. In fact, masturbation is a great way to get to know yourself and be comfortable with your body *before* you share it with somebody else.

Gal to Gal

"Wait until you are ready. Nobody is worth throwing away your first time. If he's really the one, he'll prove it to you by waiting."
—Ciara, 19

"If you can't talk comfortably about it—whatever it is—you shouldn't do it!"
—Laine, 15

"It's your body; it's all you have. Don't give it away—value it, treasure it, and respect it."
—JoJo, 18

"Think about the consequences ahead of time before you find out you are pregnant at sixteen, like I did."
—Michelle, 18

"Use protection 100 percent of the time. Believe me, the last thing you want is an STD. It can happen to you, and it's with you long after the relationship ends, a constant reminder of a bad choice."
—Claire, 19

Hey, it's okay to:

- Be curious about a physical relationship, even if you aren't emotionally ready for one.
- Be confused about the right thing to do. My advice: wait until you *do* know. Nobody ever regretted waiting, remember?
- Be the last virgin in your group. So what?
- Have already had sex, even if you regretted it. Just learn from it, sistah!
- Blush when your teacher whips out a banana to demonstrate how to use a condom in sex ed. It freaked *me* out, and I'm still uncomfortable eating bananas!
- Be more into girls than guys, or into both at once.

-Stay tuned for Lesson 6, a crash course in all things school-related—you know, like how to study smart, improve your test-taking skills, and take stock of your school career … and have fun while you are at it!

Lesson 6:
Educated Gal 101

I love smart gals! Seriously, these trying-to-be-dumb, bubble-headed, robo girls just don't do a thing for me. I think it rocks when girls are educated, street smart, up to date on current events, have an opinion on things, and can hold their own in conversations. That is empowering! So is trying your best at school, taking an interest in your education, and working towards a great future for yourself.

"I never let schooling interfere with my education."
—Mark Twain, American humorist, writer

Ahh, high school. A ton of stuff pops into my mind when I think of it. Studying, endless hours of homework, pressure, stress, drama. But there are good things, too, like working towards my future, fun, learning, friends, interesting subjects, and the countdown to graduation. See, it isn't all bad! I don't know about you, but I actually liked school. I *lived* for my English and writing classes. I couldn't get enough of them! It was in fifth grade, with one of the best teachers in the world, when I realized I loved to write. I wrote a poem about my pet goat called "Bilbo, the Singing Goat," and not only did I get an A on it, I got to have it displayed on the Wall of Honor. That's right, my first taste of celebrity! It was then that I realized that my words could affect people, and I was hooked! I wasn't the best student, but I wasn't the worst, and I tried my best, which I felt mattered most. I found something I loved and took advantage of the opportunity to learn more about it, and it's grown into something I'm really proud of. Being able to go to school and learn is a privilege, and it's up to you how much or how little you get out of it. You don't have to be the smartest or the best; you just have to take responsibility for your education and your future, and make the best decisions for you. Before we get into all the learning glory, here's another li'l quiz for you!

What's Your Educated-Gal IQ?

1 = No way; 2 = Sorta, sometimes; 3 = Sure do!

	1	2	3
1) I take my school career seriously.	1	2	3
2) I totally intend to stay in school, no matter what.	1	2	3
3) I write down everything I need to do and remember.	1	2	3
4) I have clear expectations for myself.	1	2	3
5) I have the support of my family to succeed.	1	2	3
6) I do whatever it takes to succeed.	1	2	3
7) I'm involved in extracurricular activities.	1	2	3
8) I eat well, get enough sleep, and manage my stress.	1	2	3
9) I have dreams that include postsecondary education.	1	2	3
10) I surround myself with positive people.	1	2	3

Now add up the numbers and find your Educated Gal IQ. **Total:** _____

Scoring:

10-15: It looks like you could use an educational makeover. Maybe you are having trouble at school, or are super-unmotivated, or just don't see the point of showing up every day. It's too bad, because trying your best at school is one of the best ways to invest in yourself and your future—and it's not that hard, either. So, you ready for a makeover?

16-22: You probably show up every day, but maybe you're not quite putting in all the effort you are capable of, or maybe you don't believe in yourself quite as much as you'd like. So, are you ready to start doing what it takes and living up to your awesome potential? Everything you need to know to make that happen is coming up.

23-30: Okay, so kudos to you; you could have written this chapter. Seems like you are aware of your potential, maybe even enjoy school, and have some goals you are working towards. Keep up the great work, and pay special attention to the tips for taking your school career to the next level and making your goals and dreams a reality.

You have your own reasons for either loving or hating school. All I want to do here is show you the importance of taking stock of your educational life and living up to your potential. Education really does open doors for you, and the better you do now, the better off you'll be down the road. You'll learn all that and more in "The Importance of an Education," along with some killer success and study tips! Then, in "College Bound," you will find a no-nonsense guide to picking a school that's right for you, and what you can do to maximize your chances of getting accepted.

The Importance of an Education

"Stay in school!" Anybody ever told you that before? I know I told you that I'd never tell you what to do, and I'm not. I'm just *suggesting* that if you want to have a career you love, money in the bank, a means to support yourself and your family, and the ability to take trips and buy new things, you should most definitely *consider* staying in school. It's up to you—if you want to drop out, make $14.50 an hour (the average wage that high school dropouts make throughout their lives), and not get your dream home, hubby, or holidays, then by all means, wave sayonara to your school and go for it! The only trouble with that is that even though $14.50 an hour sounds pretty good right now, it

won't go very far when you have a couple kids, a mortgage, and car payments.

You are in school for you—not your mom or dad, teachers, or friends. The time and effort you put into school is an investment in you. You can either keep investing in your future, or you can cash out. It may seem like a good idea now—you won't have to deal with cliques, pressure, tests, or due dates—but if you take the easy way out, you will pay later. Take it from a friend of mine, who wrote these words to share with you:

I was one of those "stupid girls." I wasn't really stupid; I just acted it. I felt school was the biggest waste of time, ever, and all my friends were older than me and making good money, working. I thought if they could do it, so could I. I was tired of spending all my time at school, getting detention, and failing my tests. So, I dropped out in tenth grade. I got a job working in a clothing store, making ten dollars an hour, and I thought I was on top of the world! I moved in with my friend, and for about six months, it was great; I'm not going to lie. But then, I got fired from my job for being late a couple times, and nobody would hire me! I had no education, no references, no money saved, and I couldn't afford to keep going out with my friends. I looked for about two months, then eventually landed a job at a gas station for $8.25 an hour. Meanwhile, all my friends still in school were living at home and didn't even have to worry about things like phone bills or electricity. It was really, really hard. So, I called my mom and asked her if I could move back in (she kicked me out when I quit school), and she said I was more than welcome but only if I enrolled back in school. I was totally bummed, but I had no choice. I didn't want to work at a gas station for the rest of my life! So, I moved home and took correspondence courses to graduate. I did way better studying at home, and I am a happy college student today! Sure, I'm a year behind my high school friends, but I'm so much farther ahead than my friends who dropped out!

Still thinking that dropping out is a good choice? You wouldn't be alone; thousands of students drop out *every single day.* But before you decide, check out these facts and stats from the Bureau of Labor Statistics:

• The average high school dropout makes $21,200 a year.

- The average high school graduate makes somewhere around $30,000 a year. (A little better, but still tough to get by.)

- The average college graduate (four years) makes almost $50,000 a year. (Yup, that's over twice as much as the high school dropout.)

- According to the Boys and Girls Clubs of America, 74 percent of teens surveyed think college is necessary to meet their career goals.

It pays (literally) to not only stay in school but to succeed in school. Giving up on it is giving up on yourself and your future. Plus, according to employers (the people who give you a paycheck), the skills you learn at school help make you a more desirable job candidate. What skills, you ask? How about these:

- **Communication skills**. Any employer will tell you that writing and speaking skills are paramount for almost every job. (Okay, maybe not miming, but you get the point.) At some point in your career, you are probably going to have to write a report, send important e-mails, or put together proposals, and you are definitely going to have to speak to your boss, co-workers, and other business professionals. Knowing how to express yourself eloquently and confidently is paramount.

- **Teamwork and leadership.** You know how it is when your teacher makes you get into groups with your classmates and work on a project or solve problems? That's to help you learn to voice your opinion, work well with others, figure out solutions, and take on leadership roles, all of which are really important in the workplace.

- **Staying calm.** Tests suck, and it's true that most employers won't make you answer questions on the Civil War for two hours at a time, but learning how to keep your cool during tests and exams will help you to not crack under the pressure of a deadline or mini-meltdown at your company.

- **Problem-solving skills.** Figuring out mega-tough algebra problems will help you to think critically, look for the best solution, and have the confidence to follow something through once you are in the workplace.

- **Honesty and integrity.** Each time you resist the urge to have somebody else do your homework, or you stop yourself from looking over at your neighbor's paper during an exam, that builds honesty and integrity, which is key to employers who give you access to personal information or insider secrets.

- **Multitasking and time management.** Once you graduate, you are pretty much getting a diploma in multitasking and time management as well! Think about it—how many adults do you know who could juggle as much as you do? Three papers due by Friday, a test on world history on Wednesday, cheerleading practice, tutoring your classmates at lunch on Tuesday, the big game on Friday, Jenny's party on Saturday, and the family dinner on Sunday! Yikes! If you can do all that, you can totally handle the pressure of everything you are going to have to deal with in the workplace.

And you thought school was pointless? It doesn't matter if you will ever use Spanish again; you will use the skills you gained by taking it, and they will help you down the road.

I hope I convinced you that school *is* important, and if you want to give yourself the best opportunity to succeed, you owe it to yourself to stick it out and do your best. Here are some tips on doing just that. Imagine that!

What You Need to Succeed

When you think of having a successful high school career, what kind of things do you think of? Good grades, good friends, getting along with teachers, trying hard, feeling proud of yourself, looking forward to your classes, doing extracurricular activities, being on your school team, contributing to your school community? Any and all of those things are part being a successful student. What follows is a ton of info to help you achieve as much success as you'd like.

Want It

If you don't want to succeed, no amount of studying, organization, or tutoring is going help you. It's not even about the grades. Sure, you have to peel your mother off the ceiling when she explodes with delight after seeing straight A's, but it's about taking control of your education, stepping up, putting in the work, and putting yourself in the best position now for the rest of your life. Dig real deep, and find that part of you that really *wants* to succeed in school—and remind yourself of it every day. You could even write it on a small piece of paper and keep it in your locker, so you see it all the time. It might be so you can get into your dream school, get a scholarship, or just to prove to yourself that you can be the first person in your family to graduate. Being self-motivated will help you make it through the classes that you really, really, really don't like, and it'll make dealing with a less-than-friendly teacher survivable, because you know you are doing it for you.

Participate in Class

Showing up is a good start, but you are still only halfway there. Believe it or not, the stuff that your teachers talk about in class is covered for a reason. The more present you are in class, the more you will learn, and the better you will do on tests and projects. After all, it's not about memorizing stuff, it's about *learning* it. So, when you are in a class discussion, raise your hand, even if it's just to ask a question. Teachers take note of who participates and who doesn't, and your effort in class plays a role in your final grade, too.

Prioritize and Manage Your Time Well

School can take a backseat to things like friends, parties, TV, Facebook, and dates. If you don't decide to make it a priority, it'll be way harder to find time to put in the effort it takes to be successful.

"I was a party girl in high school. Me and my friends went to every party, threw our own, and were known as a good time. Unfortunately, partying and having fun were the only things I cared about. My grades got really bad, and I just didn't care. I ended up failing history, and I didn't get my diploma on stage with everybody else. I had to go to summer school, which sucked! I ended up getting a job [from] my uncle, which is okay. I just can't help but wonder what my life would be like if I'd made the extra effort and got my priorities straight."
—Caitlin, 22

Managing your time is an essential skill when it comes to being a successful gal at school. That's why knowing your priorities is so important. If you feel you have no time to do anything, you might be surprised where you can pick up a whole bunch of extra hours a week. Did you know that if you watch just one hour less of TV every day, cut your Internet use back by thirty minutes, and take another thirty minutes off your daily texting and messaging, you'll gain an extra fourteen hours a week? Think what you could do with that!

Fill out this chart to see how much time you waste each week:

TV watching = _____ hours
Internet = _____ hours
Phone calls/texting = _____ hours
Other = _____ hours
Total = _____

It's like adding a couple extra hours a day, right? Next time you think you don't have time to study, do your homework, or join the Mathletes, think again! Time management is a super-important skill to develop now, because in the real world, baby, it gets a whole lot crazier!

Get and Stay Organized

This one didn't come easy to me in high school. I was the one with loose leaf from math class in her French binder, and a backpack full of papers from who knows where. You can take it from me that being unorganized is so not effective, and it only takes an hour, tops, to get things in place at home and at school.

The other cool thing about being organized is that your brain becomes instantly less cluttered as well. Now, if I'm feeling a little crazy, I look around me; chances are that things are out of order. As soon as I clean them up, life is clear again, and I can get back to work.

The time it takes to get organized is so worth it. It actually saves time in the long run because you know where everything is, and you have a clear space to do your homework so you don't put it off, which gets you more and more stressed out.

Organizing Your Locker, Binders, Work Station

1) Take everything out and start with a clean slate. It's probably a good idea to do it before or after school, when there are fewer people around, and you have a little more time. You could even recruit a couple friends to help out, just as long as you return the favor later on.

2) Make a couple piles. Depending on what you are organizing, you could have a "keep" pile, a "garbage" pile, and a "donate" pile. When it comes to your binders, organize all the loose papers into their appropriate sections like "algebra," "multiplication," etc. If in doubt about anything, throw it out. If you haven't used it in the last six months, throw it out. The chances are if you can live without it for six months, you can live without it, period.

3) Set up a system that works for you. This may be a filing system that you place in your locker or on your desk at home that is labeled and easy to use. Make it as easy as possible, so that you don't even have to think about doing any of it. It should be second nature to you after a while. Do what makes sense. If you have to force yourself to do it, you won't do it.

4) Stay on top of it. Now that it's all done, make sure you keep it up, instead of sliding back into Clutterville. As life goes on, more important things come up and the filing system and all the good intentions that went along with it suddenly may be forgotten. Keep a checklist in your locker or on your desk that you go over each day. It could be something like this:

> ✔ *All loose-leaf paper put in correct location*
> ✔ *All homework is where it should be*
> ✔ *Pens, pencils, and erasers in container*
> ✔ *All food removed (along with dirty gym clothes)*
> ✔ *All garbage in the garbage*

5) Organize other areas of your life as well, as long as you are at it and all! By now, you should have your binder, locker, and desk all squeaky clean, so what about the rest of your life? Are your clothes all folded up or hung in your closet? Can you actually see your floor? Set aside time this weekend to do a total room organization.

Study Smart

Studying is kind of an art in itself. Nobody is born wanting to sit down for hours to figure out exactly where you carry the seven or what "x" really stands for. Great studiers are made, not born, my friend. And here's how you, too, can exercise your study muscle all the way to a 4.0 GPA—or at least make it a little less like torture and a little more like … well, studying.

Create Study Space

As tempting as it is to do your homework in your bed, it's just not going to cut it. Having a place in your room or house that is just for studying and homework will help you get in that "homework frame of mind," and that will help you focus, stay on task, and help all the info sink in a whole lot better. Here are the elements of a good study space:

- **A desk.** Make sure it's big enough to fit all your stuff, but small enough that everything is within reach.
- **Comfy chair.** You are going to be spending a couple hours a night in it, so make sure it's comfy and adjusted appropriately. That will make you way more comfortable and less fidgety.
- **Supplies.** Pens, pencils, erasers, loose-leaf and scrap paper, a computer or laptop, a glass of water (your brain works better when it's hydrated), and a calculator should all be easily accessible so you don't have to waste time looking for stuff.
- **Light.** Good lighting is super-important to keep you alert and to make sure your eyes aren't straining to read your notes and textbooks. Too bright, and you'll get a headache; too dull, and you'll fall asleep.
- **Background noise.** Some people work better with background noise; others get distracted by it. Do whatever you prefer. Playing slow tempo, relaxing, or classical music are good choices if you dig noise in the background.

Schedule Study Time

Whether you are doing homework or studying, having "work time only" is an important way to make sure you get stuff done and stay focused on what you are doing (and not daydreaming about Chris Brown). Giving yourself blocks of study time, like from 5:00 to 6:00, followed by a fifteen break. Then study again from 6:15 to 7:00, etc. You will be way more effective than just studying when you "feel like it," which, in my experience, is usually never.

If you have a short attention span—and let's face it; who doesn't?—try studying for shorter periods of time and then having short breaks to stretch and eat and enjoy life.

EG Tip: Keep a bottle or glass of water next to you, along with some healthy snacks you can munch on to keep you hydrated and fueled up. Plus, you won't have an excuse to run to the kitchen every time you get stumped!

Study on the Go

Is it just me, or are flash cards one of the best inventions ever? You can write the question on the front, the answer(s) on the back, and take them everywhere with you. They were one of my keys to success in school. And if your friends make flash cards as well, you can switch and try other people's questions … which brings me to my next point.

Get Your Friends Involved

It's always easier to do things when they are fun, and getting your friends together to study is a great idea to help you feel more prepared for the class or test. Grab some pals and set up a study group. Maybe you could meet one or two times a week and borrow each other's brains for an hour or two. Keep these guidelines in mind, though.

- Set a strict time line. When you are working in groups, it's so easy to get distracted and start goofing off. Instead, set aside a two-hour period, and within that period, divide each subject you want to study into blocks. Allow a five- to ten-minute break between each one.
- Appoint a group leader to keep everybody focused and on task and to make sure everything gets covered.
- Plan to meet at least once a week, and if you are having a particularly tough time with a subject, ask a teacher to spend thirty minutes with your group to help everybody out.

"I used to be really into doing my own work and not relying on other people to help me out. But my friend started a study group to prepare for the SATs and invited me to join. It was so helpful. And it was really cool to hear people my own age explain stuff in a language I actually understood. instead of trying to figure it out on my own"
—Elizabeth, 17

If studying in groups proves too distracting for you, it might be good to consider getting a "study buddy" instead. A study buddy is somebody you can share notes with, trade flash cards with, meet with once or twice a week, and help to stay motivated. Here are some things to consider when choosing a study buddy. He or she should:

- Be in most of the same classes as you.
- Have similar study habits, grades, and goals as you.
- Be reliable and hard-working—like you.

Keep these tips and strategies in mind. Whether you study alone, in a group, or with a buddy, keep up the hard work, put in the effort, and you will have a way better chance of making the grade.

But what about tests? Those can make or break your school career. Here's what you need to know to keep your cool, get prepared, and psych yourself up, not out.

Test and Exam Tips

- Talk to your teachers about important info. If you make the extra effort to meet with your teachers, they will probably give you some inside tips on what to study or what to go over.
- Most of the big exams, like the SATs in the States and the "Provincials" in Canada, have past exams available for students. Ask your teacher, or search online, and take a few of them, as if they were real. Yup, that means closed book and only a couple bathroom breaks!
- Find out beforehand how the questions will be structured (for example, multiple choice, short answers, long answers, essay questions, true or false, or interpretive dance). Knowing what to expect will help you feel confident about the test before you take it.
- Think positive! When I was at school, many, many years ago (okay, four), I remember fellow students freaking themselves out by saying they were gonna fail, that they were stupid, that they "just don't get it," and that they would rather get a lobotomy than take the test. They'd be so stressed out and psyched out that they would do really bad on the test. On the other hand, if you think positive, chill out, and stay calm, your brain will work a whole lot better.
- Read over the test, front to back, before you start it, and ask your teacher for clarification on any questions you don't understand. Then, start on the hardest questions first, leaving the true-or-false or multiple-choice questions for the end.
- Have a good night's sleep before the test. As tempting as it is to cram your brain full of trinomials the night before, you probably won't remember much the next day, so give yourself an early night so you wake up feeling refreshed and less stressed.
- Eat breakfast—that's super-important. Even if you aren't hungry in the morning, grabbing a quick bite will feed your brain and help you concentrate.

- Don't be too hard on yourself. If you honestly try your very best but end up with a low score, be proud of yourself. Just make sure you schedule a meeting with your teacher to talk about what you can do to improve or how to get extra help or extra credit to make up for it.

See? Studying doesn't have to be so mind-numbingly dull or stressful or take up every moment of spare time.

Get Help If You Need It (Extra Credit Helps, Too!)

- Make friends with your teachers—be friendly and say hello. Believe it or not, they aren't out to get you, and if you are friendly, they will be more willing to help you.
- Get a tutor. Some classes are just too tough to struggle through on your own if you don't get the material. See if your school offers a tutoring program, hire a college student to help you, or check out one of the many after-school tutoring programs available in your community or online. Also, a lot of teachers supplement their income by tutoring, so ask around.
- Ask for and do the extra credit. It really does make a difference and can easily bump you up a grade or two.
- If you had trouble on the homework, show up to class early to get some help. That way, your teacher knows you care, and you'll get some one-on-one help. Plus, it beats showing up to class without your homework complete!

Being a successful student is about more than just grades; it's about the whole package. If you want to succeed, you have to make an effort. Try your best, get help when you need it, and do whatever it takes— you have a lot to be proud of.

But what about the world outside your classroom?

Outside School Education: It's a Good Thing

Sure, we learn a lot of great stuff at school, but it's not the beginning and the end of our educational lives. There is a great big world outside the four walls of your classroom, which you will be very aware of the moment you throw your cap into the air and think to yourself, "Now what?" Here are some ways to keep yourself educated outside of school, make learning fun, bond with your friends, and de-stress.

- Read one nonfiction book each month on a topic of your choice. It could be business, self-help, psychology, or nature. Spend an afternoon browsing the local bookstore or online and find books that interest you.
- Read the newspaper at least once a week. This one is still hard for me, but when I do accomplish it, I get that worldly, cultured feeling one seems to get from reading a newspaper. Plus, you'll learn what's going on in your community, find volunteer opportunities, and be inspired to help causes that are important to you.
- Travel somewhere you've never been before. This doesn't mean hopping on a plane to Nairobi, but it does mean packing your car full of friends and heading to the state across from yours—or even a nearby town. Or, how about visiting a historic site or doing a summer-abroad program? It's more about meeting new people, seeing new things, and experiencing stuff you've never done before.
- Your nearby college, university, or adult-education programs have tons of seminars on all different topics. Visit their Web sites to check out any upcoming events that interest you, and drag a pal along with you. You could hone your sewing skills for the next great fashion line or learn something totally random, like yodeling!
- Pack a lunch and head to a nearby park or outdoor area. Sit quietly, watch nature, and contemplate life.
- Go to a local museum or historical site and find out a little bit about your city or town.
- Do research on artists or musicians who inspire you, and see if you can create your own work of art.
- Visit your grandparents or other elderly family members, and listen to their stories. Not only will this mean the world to them, but you also will gain insight into your family's history and the kind of world they grew up in.
- Volunteer for a cause you believe in. Whether it is the local nursing home or the animal-rescue society, you'll meet lots of interesting people and learn so much about yourself and the causes you are helping.
- Ask to go to work with one of your parents on a day off school. You'll gain insight into the real world of work, find out what Mom or Dad actually does all day, and see what you like or dislike about that particular job. It'll help you narrow down what it is you want to do for a living.

College Bound

"I am _so_ excited for college. Freedom here I come!"
—Melissa, 18

"I just got accepted into my dream school, and it's the coolest feeling ever. My parents are so proud of me, and now I get to start working toward the rest of my life. All the hard work in high school was totally worth it!"
—Jen, 17

"All my friends are excited, but I'm pretty nervous. I've never been away from my family before, and I'm not sure I am ready. I hope by the beginning of September, I feel differently!"
—Amanda, 17

Whether you are a freshman or senior, you have undoubtedly given some thought to college, or at least to what you are going to do after high school. You might be super-excited ("Hello! My own dorm room, cool roommates, parties, college guys, _freedom_!"). Or you might be a little more reluctant ("I'm going to miss my friends and my parents! I can't afford to pay! What if I can't get in?"). Or you might fall somewhere in the middle. No matter what, it's a time in your life that is going to really begin shaping the _rest_ of your life. The decisions you make regarding whether or not to go to college, which institution you choose, and what you are going to study are all going to impact your life.

I'm totally not trying to freak you out, but this is a really big step for you to embrace and really think about. Pulling a "Felicity" (following your dream guy off to whatever college he chooses) is not a good enough way to decide. But before we get into this college talk any further, I have a confession to make: I never went to college. (Now, watch me never get booked at another school for the rest of my life!) Here's why:

I remember sitting in Mrs. Elliot's second-grade class at Yarrow Elementary School. All my teachers always told me that I was going to make a great teacher one day, and so I thought that, yeah, I'd be a teacher. But when I was watering my bean plant on the ledge of the chalkboard, I had a mini-meltdown. I just *knew*, deep down inside, that I wasn't going to college. I just felt it, felt that there were other plans for my life. And I felt I was going to let everybody down. It wasn't until years later, when I started my business, that I realized that college wasn't for me *right now*. I've enrolled in online courses and am studying English Lit and stuff like that, but I didn't feel I needed or wanted the experience of actually going to college. I had really big dreams with my business and the opportunity to pursue them. I couldn't imagine waiting four years until I could do what I was most passionate about. So, not going to college has worked for me, but the odds were stacked against me. I took a major risk by putting my college money into my business, and it paid off, but lots of times it doesn't.

The bottom line here is, no matter what choice you make, you have to own it, see it from every angle, and be prepared to face the consequences. The consequences of my having made a wrong decision would have been pretty rough. But I'm pretty determined, and I felt in the deepest part of my soul that my business was my passion, purpose, and bliss. It would be hypocritical of me to say you *must* go to college, so all I can suggest is to follow your bliss, wherever it leads you.

How to Know If College Is for You
- You have absolutely no idea of what you'd like to do with your life.
- The career (and lifestyle) you covet most requires a degree or postsecondary education (most careers do, especially the ones that pay well).
- You are terrified about the real world at this point and want to put it off for at least another four years.
- You have dreamed about experiencing college life for as long as you can remember.
- Your room is wallpapered with flags, posters, and pictures of your dream college.
- You are terrified by the thought of being the "daughter" part of "Ted and Daughter's Super Plumbing."

How to Know If Something Else Is Better Right Now
- You want to travel the world and have the opportunity and finances to do so.
- Your dream career doesn't require a PhD, and you have the opportunity to start it right out of high school.
- You know what you want from life, have a great internship or career lined up, and you can't wait four years to get started on it.

- The thought of hanging out with thousands of "drunk college kids" doesn't please you one little bit.
- You have a trade school, music academy, beauty school, or Broadway calling your name.
- You want to take a year off to volunteer in a third-world country and think about what you want to do with your life before jumping in with both feet.
- All you've ever wanted is to be the "daughter" in your dad's "Ted and Daughter's Super Plumbing" company.

It's totally up to you, but either way, you *must* finish high school first! There is no way around that one, baby. If I had no idea what I wanted to do, I would be sitting in a classroom right now, trying to figure it out. I have friends in college who are loving it and having the time of their lives. They are getting degrees that will help them become very successful in the future. I also have friends who tried college for a year, found out what they really wanted to do, and left to go do it. I even have friends who are off traveling the world, four years after they graduated, experiencing an entirely different kind of education.

There are a lot of people who will tell you that you must go to college or university in order to succeed, and there are plenty of facts to back that up. People with degrees tend to, on average, make more money than those of us who don't have degrees. But it really is up to you; it's a matter of following your bliss.

Choosing a School That's Right for You

With the thousands of postsecondary options available to you, how do you pick the one that's right for you? Here are some things to consider:

- **Location.** Do you want to be close to home or as far away as you can get? In a busy city or a small, college town? Do you want to go somewhere warm or cold? Do you want to go to a different country or stay in your own?
- **Programs.** What schools are leaders in the areas you want to study? Which ones have the best reputation of producing leaders in your dream field?
- **Size.** Do you want to go to a big, super-school, or would you prefer more one-on-one attention at a smaller institution?

- **Mandatory subjects.** Each school has different core subjects that every student must take, as well as mandatory subjects that go along with your chosen major. If you are so not into the mandatory advanced physics classes, you might want to see what other schools have to offer.
- **Money.** Money should never be the reason you don't do something. There is always a way around it, even if you think your dream school is too expensive. Did you know that millions of dollars of grant and scholarship money go unused every year? There are hundreds of schools, organizations, charities, corporations, and trusts that would love to give you money! Go online, talk to your guidance counselor, or call up your dream school's financial department, and see what they have to say. Bottom line—apply for everything!

Here are some tips from girls who have made their college decision and picked a school:

"I went to every college and career fair I could to make sure I understood my options."
—Kellis, 18

"I spent hours online narrowing down my career choices and trying to find a school that would work for me."
—Ana, 18

"What worked for me was talking to adults who had my dream careers about what schools they went to and what they recommended for me."
—Jules, 18

"My parents helped me a lot. They both went to college, and they told me what they liked and didn't like from their respective colleges, and it help me make my decision."
—Miley, 19

"Once I narrowed my choices down to three, I went and visited their campuses. It was the only way for me to make the best decision."
—Fran, 20

"I went to a buddy day, where you shadow a student for a whole day, go to classes with her, etc. It gave me a way better idea about what college was like, and I got to see if the vibe of the school fit for me."
—Andrea, 19

"Congratulations!" Tips on Getting Accepted

When I put a message out on MySpace to ask girls their number-one question about school, most of the responses were along the lines of "How do I get into a good college? Please help me!"

- **Really want it!** Pick a school you are passionate about and a line of work you are super-psyched about, and don't be afraid to let it shine through. Passion goes a long way, and schools take that into consideration. (After all, who would want a campus full of kids who hated being there?) But passion, unfortunately, isn't the only thing they look for.

- **Get good grades.** Sure, they aren't the be all and end all of your school career, but they do influence your postsecondary options, probably more than anything else. But even if you don't have a 4.0 GPA, don't worry. It's not the only thing schools look at. They care about what classes you took (advanced calculus, anyone?). Since AP courses are pretty close to college-level classes, taking a couple AP courses shows you are willing to work hard and put in the extra effort, which they like. They also look at how you've improved. If you are less than stellar in the grades department, plan a meeting with your teachers, and see what you can do to improve. Extra credit, anyone?

- **Extracurricular activities.** Get involved in stuff outside of school. It looks good in your transcripts, and it'll help you build valuable skills that will make you a more desirable candidate.

- **Test scores (SAT/Provincials).** If tests aren't your thing, try not to freak out too much. If you have awesome grades, and you bomb a little on the SATs, it's not all over. But if you have average grades and you perform really well on the SATs, that could help you a ton.

- **Application and essay.** If you don't have the best grades in town, an incredible essay and application can still get you accepted, so make sure you put a ton of effort into it, and try your very best. Let them see your personality and convince them they *must* accept you!

- **Letters of recommendation.** Just like getting a reference for a job, schools want to have other people tell them how awesome you are. So, mix it up a bit. If your governor wants to write you a letter, awesome, but also focus on people like teachers, employers, and family friends, who actually know you and can rave about you from personal experience.

Start looking into colleges now. Find those that seem interesting and exciting to you, request info from them, and then make an appointment with your school counselor. Take a look at the applications early, so you know what to expect, and start thinking about visiting a couple campuses. Even if you are a freshman or sophomore, picking a school you are interested in and setting a goal to get there could really help you focus and put in the hard work you need to give yourself the best possible chance of acceptance. For more info, visit www.gocollege.com.

Gal to Gal

"One thing that kept me going through high school was keeping my eye on the prize. I knew what I wanted (to be a journalist). and it kept me motivated to keep going."
　—Mora, 21

"Well. my mom always told me to do my best. not try my best. So. I always did the very best I could. and it made a difference. I got into a great college!"
　—Ash, 19

"Write everything down! I was one of those people who would just try to remember stuff (I thought agendas were kind of lame—oops!). and I'd always forget when stuff was due. have to study last minute for tests I forgot about. and miss out on meetings and practices. As soon as I started to actually write notes to myself. it made all the difference in the world!"
　—Meg, 17

"Just show up every day. I used to skip classes because I didn't like the teachers. subjects or classmates. and my grades went way down. I was failing lots of my classes. even though I knew I was smart enough. Anyway. I eventually got my act together and showed up. and that made all the difference in the world!"
　—Polly, 18

"If you can't take regular school. instead of dropping out or skipping class and failing. do home schooling."
　—Kimmy, 16

Hey, it's okay to:

- Actually like high school. I know—gasp—but the more you try to like it, the better you will do. It's science. Or something.

- Treat your hallways like runways, showing off your stellar sense of style. Who said school can't be fun?

- Like your teachers. Most of them are actually pretty cool. I still keep in touch with lotsa mine.

- Not get straight A's. Some of us are blessed with street smarts, not necessarily school smarts. Just try your best, and you'll be fine.

- Get help when you need it. It could make all the difference. Why struggle when you don't have to?

- Stay tuned for your guide to major career success. I know, I know, you are still in high school, but as you'll find out, it's never too early to start thinking about the rest of your life, so see you there, and we'll get our career on!

Lesson 7:
Career Gal 101

This entire chapter is dedicated to helping you figure out what you want to do with the *rest of your life*. No, don't be freaked; hang on a sec. As the old folks say, you *are* pretty lucky to have your whole life ahead of you, and it's never too early to start discovering what you want to do with it. You can do anything, be anybody, achieve whatever you want, and spend your life doing something you love to do. Why not, right?

"*We are responsible for our own fate. we reap what we sow. we get what we give. we pull in what we pull out. I know these things for sure.*"
—Madonna

There is no better feeling than getting out of bed every morning and being excited to do your job. It's never too early to start figuring out what you love to do, what you are passionate about, and making goals to get there. Whether you want to get a summer or after-school job, start your own business, work your way up to the top of a Fortune 500 company, or take over the family business, there are certain tips, strategies, and qualities that will help you succeed, no matter what you want to do, be, and achieve. But first, here's another quiz to help you figure out your Career Gal IQ. But you already knew that—and the part about choosing a 1, 2, or 3.

What's Your Career Gal IQ?

1 = No way; 2 = Sorta, sometimes; 3 = Sure do!

	1	2	3
1) I have a good work ethic.	1	2	3
2) I am self-motivated to get things done.	1	2	3
3) I go above and beyond what is expected of me.	1	2	3
4) I have a clear idea of what I want to achieve.	1	2	3
5) I know what I want to do with my life.	1	2	3
6) My friends think I'll be perfect for my dream job.	1	2	3
7) I have my family's support and encouragement.	1	2	3
8) I believe in myself and my goal, 100 percent.	1	2	3
9) I believe I can work hard for my goal and achieve it.	1	2	3
10) I have an action plan and clear vision for my future.	1	2	3

Now add up the numbers and find your Career Gal IQ.   **Total:**

Scoring:

10-15: To say you are in a "career slump" is an understatement! But you're a teen, so it's no biggie; you are allowed to have no clue! You have lots of time to think about your future, but why not start now?

16-22: It looks like you've thought about what you want to do with your life and might have some ideas about how to get there. Still, you could probably use some tips and advice on getting from where you are to where you want to be.

23-30: Look at you, Little Miss Career Girl! You know your strengths and what kind of job/career you're into, and you have the skills and drive to pull it off.

The cool thing is that you have a couple of years until you really have to make big decisions about your career. Right now, you can start experimenting with jobs, try a few out after school or during the summer, and start researching careers that interest you. The first section in this chapter is all about "Jobs in High School," how to find ones that work for you, and how to get them. In "Job Skills You Need to Have," you'll learn all about acing an interview and how to make yourself irreplaceable at work. Then, I'll talk about thinking ahead to the kind of career you want to have when you are finished with school, and even how to start your own business, in "Career Planning: Finding Your Passion."

Jobs in High School

"Ever since I was a little girl I wanted to be a doctor. I remember seeing how they saved my little brother, and I wanted to do that for other families. So, I'm in my second year of med school, and I'm happier than ever. It's a lot of hard work, but I know it'll be so worth it in the end when I can do the same for other families."
—Karla (MD!), 25

"I don't know what I want to do with my life at all! Most of my friends do, or they at least know what they want to study. I'm so freaked out—I graduate in two weeks!"
—America, 17

"My parents have their own business, so I'm thinking I might want to do that as well one day. For the time being, though, I am going to start working for them so I understand what it takes and see if I could really do it on my own."
—Ash, 17

"Everybody in my family is in the restaurant business, but I have zero interest in that! They expect me to follow in their footsteps, but I really want to work at a magazine in New York one day. I'm not sure what to do."
—Mercedes, 18

Whether it is an after-school job, a summer job, or working for your parents here and there, there are some major pluses to working. You will gain valuable experience that makes you more appealing to future colleges and employers, and you also will make money and learn the value of a dollar. Believe me, when you are making your own money, it'll make it a lot easier for you to know the difference between *needing* and *wanting* stuff (especially when it comes to things like shoes). You are also figuring out what you are good at, what you enjoy doing, and what you would sooner die than ever do again.

When the time comes for you to get out there and get some work experience, here are some things you need to ask yourself:

- *What is my motivation?* Do you need to make some money to take care of yourself or to help out your family, or do you just want the experience? If it's for the money, then definitely seek out a job that pays well and will give you the hours that you need to actually rack up some coin. If you don't really need the money, then find a job in the field that you are most interested in.

- *What would I do for free because I love it so much?* Are you a fashion junkie, or are you so dog-crazy you decorated your room with "Dogs of the World" wallpaper? Your cue for finding a great job should start with doing something you actually enjoy, even if you are just working in a clothing store or walking dogs. If you love it, you'll get way more out of it and put way more into it, which impresses employers.

- *What are my long-term goals?* Have you wanted to run a business ever since you were old enough to say "You're fired" in your best Donald Trump impersonation, or have you always wanted to be a dancer on tour with your favorite singer? If you have a mega-interest in a certain area, look for a job that in some way relates to it to get your foot in the door, and figure out if it's something you could see yourself doing for the rest of your life.

Find Your Perfect Job—Fast!

Use this snazzy little form to get a better idea of what kind of job you want. Fill in the blanks with the information that best fits you right now.

Do you want to work part time or full time? _____

Do you want to work inside or outside? _____

What do you enjoy doing? (For example, cooking, cleaning, food prep, organizing, answering phones, computer work, customer service, waiting tables)_____

How many hours would you like to work?
     ___ hours a day ___ days a week

How much money do you hope to make? At least $_____/hour *(Expect to make at least minimum wage. Check your state or province requirements for teen wages, as they vary from place to place.)*

Now that you have a better idea of what you are looking for, here are some tips to finding the kind of job that works for you:
- Research your dream job. Find out what's out there and available, and what you think you'll be good at.
- Ask friends or family if they know of any openings at their or their friend's places of work that would suit you. The bonus here is that you get an instant reference and have a foot in the door.
- Go online. There are so many job sites online these days, but two popular sites for young people are www.craigslist.com and www.monster.com.
- Check the classified ads in your local paper.
- If you can't find a job opening that suits you, try going to your ideal place of work and talk to the owner or manager. Try your hand at convincing that person that he or she needs you. Bring your résumé, if you have one; if not, bring a page or two of personal references from family, family friends, teachers, etc., and a winning attitude, and tell the person in charge why you'd love to work there. Say that you'll start anywhere, even sweeping the floor, to get your foot in the door. The pay might not be great, but if it's the experience you are after, it'll be worth it.
- Always have a friend or family member go with you when meeting somebody for the first time about a job or career opportunity, and stay clear of those "get rich quick" schemes all over the Internet. Remember, if it sounds too good to be true, it probably is.

Here are some popular part-time and summer jobs for teens. Find the perfect one for you now.

If you like being outdoors:

- Tourist Attractions. Usually busiest in the summer and on most school holidays. Most cities or towns have at least one attraction, so if you enjoy being outside and learning more about your community, this would be a good job for you. Call or visit your local tourist info center to see what's available.
- Parks and Recreation Centers. Usually have openings for students to help run special programs, especially during the summer when they are busiest. Visit your local park district headquarters, in person or online, and look for openings.
- Summer Camps. What is better than going to summer camp? Getting paid to go! If you went to a camp as a kid, you'll know how much fun it is, and if you like being outside and working with kids, this could be the perfect opportunity to gain work experience and make some extra cash.
- Sports Clubs. If you love golf or tennis, this would be perfect for you, especially in the summer, when many are looking for part-time help.

If you like shopping, clothes, and fashion:

- Retail Stores in the Mall. Chances are, if you are a fan you know a ton about the products, what the stores sell, and the kinds of people they are selling to, so who better to work there? Plus, you will get a discount on merchandise—it's a win/win, just as long as you don't spend your entire paycheck on their merch!
- Small Businesses and Boutiques. You will be especially appealing to small-business owners who usually look for part-time help that doesn't cost a fortune. Plus, you will get a ton of hands-on experience on what it takes to run a business. Pick one in a field you are already interested in to get the most out of it.

If you work well with people:

- Restaurants. Whether or not it's fast food, restaurant work usually requires some training and provides you with great experience in customer service, or if you prefer, food prep.
- Hotels and Resorts. Especially popular in the summer, but they require help all year round. Hotels and resorts are a great if you

enjoy working with and meeting new people. Consider a job at the front desk or taking bookings.

- Grocery Stores. It might not seem very exciting, but it's great if you want to acquire responsibility that isn't too heavy and have some extra cash in your pocket. And most towns have at least one grocery store!

Job Skills You Need to Have:

"I was so nervous when I went to my first interview, but I just remembered to stay calm and just be myself. It worked, because I got the job!"
—Cara, 17

Your classes probably cover factoring trinomials, the history of Ancient Egypt, and the life cycle of salmon. But do you learn one of the essential life skills—job skills —for the gal on the go? It's sad but true: most of the time, you don't get a crash course in them until you actually have a job.

It takes more than a winning attitude to get the job. You have to have a killer résumé (with previous work experience, volunteer activities, extracurricular activities, school achievements, your skills and strengths, and a couple great references). You need to ace the interview, show enthusiasm, and learn your job. Sounds tough, but let's break it down, starting with the interview. It might be scary, but if you are prepared, it will go a whole lot smoother.

Here's what you need to know to ace your interview:
- Know what the company wants by doing a little research, and think about how you can best meet the needs of the company.
- Walk in there like you already have the job—super-confident!
- Be passionate about the job! Don't be afraid to let your future boss know how much you'd love the job and how hard you'd work if you had the opportunity to join the team.
- Be early! Not only will it look good, but you'll be able to sit and chill out for a few minutes, relax, or go to the ladies room and fix yourself up a bit.
- Bring an extra copy of your résumé with you in case the first one you sent got lost.
- Dress for success *and* the position. Look polished, sophisticated, and like you fit in at the company.

- Practice a nice, firm handshake—not bone-crushing, but not floppy, either.
- Greet everybody in the room with a big smile, and be friendly.
- Research the industry and know your stuff.
- Make eye contact, sit up straight, and don't fidget.
- Be honest, but don't shoot yourself in the foot. It's okay to keep the office romance at your last job a secret.
- Don't get flustered. Stay cool, calm, and collected. Freak out *after* you leave!

Whether or not you get the job, send a thank-you card, note, or e mail after the interview. This speaks volumes to a potential employer and will keep you fresh in his or her mind if an appropriate opening comes up for you. Don't get discouraged if you don't get the job. You might have made a great impression, but you just weren't right for that particular job, and you might get a call when the right job for you becomes available.

Mastering the "Greatest Weakness" Question

Talk about a trick question! Almost all potential employers seem to ask this during an interview: "What's your greatest weakness?" Well, I'm going to let you in on a little secret. They don't really want you to tell them your greatest weakness. If you are a chronic bed-wetter, you can keep that to yourself. You also might not want to tell them that you have ADHD, can't keep a straight face when somebody falls down (guilty!), or don't complete a project until the morning before it's due. What they are really checking for is how well you think on your feet and how well you can turn it into a positive. Try something like this:

- "Well, I am super-concerned with getting the job done and when I'm working on a project, it tends to come before anything else."
- "My friends tell me that I put others' satisfaction before my own and try really hard to make sure everybody around me is happy."
- "I spend too much time volunteering." Okay, so only use this one as a joke if you feel comfortable and the vibe of the interview is right. Follow it up with something like, "No, actually, as much as I love to volunteer, I think my greatest weakness is being a perfectionist."

You might want to avoid giving a response like this:
- "I am so attractive that people, like, don't take me seriously."
- "Umm, well, I don't know. I guess I might be, sort of, indecisive. But I'm not sure if that is true or not."
- "I usually can't see a project through. I don't really care about customer service. Hey, how many days do I get off at Christmas?"

"I've always been a big believer in equality. No one has ever been able to tell me I couldn't do something because I was a girl."
–Anne Hathaway, actress

Public Profiles

For the sake of argument, let's just assume that everybody's potential boss knows what MySpace and Facebook are all about. When you are putting up pics of your crazy spring-break trip, ask yourself, "What does this say about me? How might this affect my future?" I can tell you right now that winning the bikini contest is not something a boss considers an award or achievement. Play it safe with public profiles. What goes online stays online, and what seemed like fun at the time could come back to hurt you later on.

EG Tip: Before you send out your résumés, Google your name and see what pops up. If there are any pics or comments that could hurt your chances, remove them before your future boss sees them!

Being a Good Employee

When you first start working, it can be hard to grasp everything that is expected of you. But no matter the scope of your job, there are certain things that employers just love. The sooner you start learning them, the better!

Be on time. This may seem like a no-brainer, but it's not as easy as it sounds. I mean, who hasn't missed the bus to school and ended up walking into math class fifteen minutes late and having the entire class look up at you like you have the plague or something? At work, that kind of thing is even less acceptable. Excuses like "I got stuck in traffic" won't cut it. Especially because the chances that everybody else was helicoptered in are a little outside the realm of possibility.

Make sure you allow for an extra ten minutes so you are at your desk, counter, etc., and ready to go when the clock strikes whatever o'clock you are supposed to be there. Bosses look for stuff like that, and it matters. Being on time shows you care, are responsible, and are a team player—all of which, by the way, goes a really long way when it comes to promotions, job opportunities, and letters of recommendation.

It is all part of your job. Even if your job title is "secretary," your job is to make everything part of your job. A business is a team working towards a common goal, and you are just as integral to that as the CEO. The farther you go above and beyond what is expected of you, the better you are going to do.

Ask, ask, and ask. Instead of spending an hour trying to figure something out, take five minutes and ask for help. Remember, you are part of a team. Movies and TV shows train us that the new employees get shot down by catty co-workers whenever they ask a question, but more often than not, if you ask politely and show a genuine interest in their advice, they will be more than willing to help you out. If not, find someone else. Trust me; you are way more of an asset if you ask questions than if you don't.

Care about detail and quality. Think of yourself, signing off on every project you do or are involved with. Your name is attached to it. Is it something you are proud of? Did you put time and effort into it? Did you try your best? Did you cut corners or not do a proper job? An expense report deserves as much attention as the fall fashion layout. If your boss sees you are detail-oriented and produce quality work, that is going to mean a lot.

Fill in the blanks. Is something missing? Does the client need some water? Does a co-worker need you to cover her for a few minutes so she can sort out a mini-crisis involving her dog, a pair of Gucci shoes, and her best friend/dog-sitter? Be the girl to fill in the missing pieces. Think ahead; what's missing? How can you prepare for the worst? What can you do to save the day?

Find solutions. If there is something wrong, everybody knows it's wrong. Instead of focusing on the problem, find solutions. Optimism is a really important quality, in life and at work. Approach every setback with a solution in mind, and you'll be irreplaceable to your company in no time!

Be passionate. Even if you are starting in the mailroom of your fave magazine, approach stuffing envelopes and delivering letters with as much passion as you would running the company! Passion and drive is what gets you noticed, and it puts you on the fast track to success. Whatever your job, bring as much passion and enthusiasm to it as you possibly can. Plus, if you like it, you'll probably be good at it!

Jobs in high school help prepare you for the real world of work—you know, the thing you spend most of your life doing? It's never too early to start thinking about your long-term career goals and figuring out what you can do now to help you get there.

"Guys will just go out and do something. Females will talk about it—a lot. ... You have to be aggressive to get the same respect as the guys."
—Mya, singer-songwriter

Career Planning: Finding Your Passion

"I followed my heart and figured that if I tried and failed, at least I'd know that I tried."
—Michelle Branch, singer-songwriter

Oprah did it, so did Hilary Duff. Maya Angelou did it. Bill Gates did it. Kimora Lee Simmons did it. And *you can, too*! Oprah turned her love of talking to people and making a difference into a billion-dollar career. Hilary Duff turned her love of performing and fashion into a multi-million-dollar business empire. Maya Angelou turned her love of words and writing into a career with a legacy that inspires millions of young girls today. Kimora Lee Simmons turned her love of fashion and edgy style into Baby Phat, a business empire that keeps growing bigger and more fabulous every season. Bill Gates turned his love of technology into ... well, Microsoft, anybody?

Doing what you love—and getting paid for it! It sounds almost too good to be true. But millions of people get up every day and actually look forward to working. Just because you may know adults who hate their jobs, complain, and wish there was another option, doesn't mean that will happen to you. Why can't you find what you love and do it?

Here's how you can:

What do you love? Use the space below to list the top five things you love to do.

1)_____

2)_____

3)_____

4)_____

5)_____

Now, brainstorm how each of those loves in your list could be turned into a career. For example, if one thing on your list is your love of dogs, you could be a dog groomer, dog sitter, or dog walker. You could design clothes for dogs, own a pet shop where you sell dogs, start a mobile dog-grooming service, bake gourmet dog treats, photograph dogs, do custom paintings of dogs, become a small-animal vet to treat dogs, or write children's books about dogs! There is no limit to where you can go with it, so take some time now, and see how you can turn the things you love the most into a career. Don't be afraid to think outside the box a little bit, and see how you can combine two or three of the things you love into a truly unique career. I'm sure nobody has ever heard of doggie dance classes, but if dog therapy took off, why not?

Use this space to name one of the loves you listed above, and brainstorm a dream career:

I love _____

Dream Career Options:

_____

_____

_____

_____

_____

_____

_____

_____

Being Young: Your Career

"Women have to harness their power—it's absolutely true. It's just learning not to take the first no. And if you can't go straight ahead, you go around the corner."
—Cher, recording artist, actress

Everybody has to start somewhere; just because you are young doesn't mean you can't be successful. A lot of girls e-mail me, telling me their really big dreams, but they think that because they are in their late teens or early twenties, people won't take them seriously. No way, girls! I know a thing or two about being young and in business, and do you want to know the cool thing? Even though I'm always the youngest one at the event, either speaking or attending, it opens up so many more doors! People take notice. They can't believe that a twenty-two-year-old is in the same game they spent twenty-two years trying to get into. Now, once the door is open, it's a different story. If you are playing with the big girls and boys who have a lifetime of experience on you, you have to prove yourself. It's a really fun challenge, but you just have to keep some things in mind in order for your boss and colleagues to take you seriously.

Starting young has been the most fantastic thing for me. Sure, I missed out on stuff like school parties and prom, but I've gotten to do such cool things because of it, like travel all over the world, meet my mentors and idols, and grow in *so* many important ways. Whether you want to start your dream business or go after your dream job at a young age, here are some do's and don'ts of getting your cute little foot in the door—and keeping it there:

Do know your stuff. You may be a novelty, and that will get people initially interested in you, but in order to keep them interested, you need to know your stuff—and then some! Research your business from top to bottom. Know the key players, trends, history, breakthroughs, publications, authors, and personalities in whatever field you want to be a part of. Keep up on current events, and know your stuff inside and out. This can be threatening for some of the insecure people who've been in the business since before you were born, and they might try to throw you off and intimidate you. But if you are a gal who knows what she is talking about and can hold her own, you'll come out on top.

Do know you deserve to be there. Just because you are young doesn't mean you are out of your league. You have just as much a right to be doing what you love as anybody else. Don't apologize for figuring it out a whole lot sooner than they did.

Do dress for success. Even if you start at the very bottom of the pile, dress like you are a somebody. Dressing with class is never as important as it is now. Sure, jeans and a T are comfy, but they don't say a lot of great things in the workplace. And when you are young and trying to prove yourself, everything about you has to convey a level of sophistication and professionalism. If your are in an uber-professional setting but nothing freaks you out as much as a pant suit, pick a classic silhouette, like a pencil skirt and a unique but understated top or shirt, and play around with the accessories—and don't forget about the heels. But keep in mind, this is *so* not to place to get all sexed up, especially if you want people to take you seriously.

Don't get into your age. I don't know why, but women "of a certain age" would sooner die than tell you how old they are. To this day, my grandmother has never told anybody how old she is. I think by now it's probably about 112, but that's not the point. The point is, if those women can keep quiet about their age, so can you. It's not that you have anything to hide, but prove yourself first, then spill it. At business events that I attend, I tell people what I do, what I've done, and what I'm working on; then, when they ask my age, I tell them. I never introduce myself with my age. And I have to admit, I do like the shocked expression on their faces when they find out!

Don't be intimidated. The first time I was ever handed a microphone was when I was twenty, standing in a room full of people I grew up wanting to be just like. It was the first time I had met any of them, and I was the youngest one in the room by about fifteen or twenty years. I was in Los Angeles, and I was by myself, after just having moved to California from a small town in Canada. I didn't know a soul. I'd packed up my little U-Haul with everything I owned and cruised down there and right into the Hyatt Regency Orange County for my first really big, really major seminar. I had spoken to groups before—groups of high school students—but this was something totally different. I put my heart and soul into it, and felt incredible afterward.

There are going to be lots of times when you will be faced with people who intimidate you because of their status, wealth, position, or name, but you have to push through it, hold your head high, and act like you are right where you are meant to be. It can be scary, but you never move forward by staying where you are.

Do know you are there for a reason. There is a reason that you landed the internship, got the job, got invited to the party, or are up on that stage. There are a million other people who aren't where you are now, so when you get discouraged and doubt your abilities, when you think you are in over your head, remind yourself that you are there for a reason. Opportunities don't present themselves to people who aren't ready for them. The person who recommended or hired you saw something in you, so own it.

What's cool about growing up at this point in history is that we get to reinvent the way things are done. For the first time, women have almost complete control over their lives and careers. If you have a dream, passion, and drive, what are you waiting for? Get your foot in the door any way you can—or go find another door if you have to; just keep trying. Prove yourself to your employer. Make yourself invaluable and become an asset as you work your way up. Being young is no reason to hold yourself back.

"My theory is that if you look confident, you can pull anything off—even if you have no clue what you are doing."
—Jessica Alba, actress

"Keep working hard and you can get anything that you want. If God gave you the talent, you should go for it. But don't think it's going to be easy. It's hard!"
—Aaliyah, singer

Starting Your Own Business

"Luck has nothing to do with it, because I have spent many, many hours, countless hours, on the court working for my one moment in time, not knowing when it would come."
—Serena Williams,
former World No. 1 professional female tennis player

Can't find a job you like? Would you rather start your own business than make money for other people? Do you have really good ideas and a work ethic and think you might be able to pull it off? I was the same way, and that's why I started my company, Empowered Gal Inc., when I was sixteen. It has been a ton of fun and has given me my dream life, and there is no reason you can't do it, too. In fact, tons of people have, like our gal Ashley Qualls, who started www.whateverlife.com.

First, here are some important skills and rules you need to know before you incorporate the next great American business.

- Find something you love to do. There is no point putting all your energy, passion, work, and enthusiasm into something unless you love and believe in it.
- Get support. It's going to be super-important to have some adult support and possibly guidance through this process.
- Educate yourself. Once you pick what kind of business you want to have, learn it inside and out, research, and read everything you can about it.
- Come up with a cute name. Be creative and fun, and make it memorable. Play around with words, pop culture, slang, or even different languages!
- Figure out how you are going to sell it. Whether you are selling your services or a product, you need to figure out who is going to buy it, and how you are going to get your product (or service) to them.
- Go for it! You never know what might happen! If you see a need for something, fill it!

Great ideas for teen businesses:
- Go online. Design sites or graphics, or build your own online magazine. It usually only costs the fee of registering a site, usually under ten dollars.

- If you have a flair for cooking, why not make custom cupcakes for neighborhood birthday parties, or bake cookies for hungry college kids who are awake at all hours of the night.
- Throw parties for neighborhood kids. Parents are stressed and would love help in this department, so develop fun theme parties that you can throw, from princess and fairy themes for girls to sports or monster themes for boys.
- If you are outdoorsy, start a biz doing garden and lawn stuff, like mowing, gardening, cleaning out garages, or organizing a yard sale. (You might offer to take a percentage of the profits as your fee.)
- If you are artsy and creative, you could sell your own designs, like funky paintings.

Be creative. Use some of these ideas, or come up with your own.

Marketing 101

Once you have your idea, you need people to find out about it. Here are some quick tips to get you started:
- Make up a super-colorful, to the point, fun brochure that advertises your service, who you are, and why the customer needs you or your product. Print it up on your home printer, and either stuff it in mailboxes around town or go door to door, introducing yourself.
- Print business cards and flyers, and leave them in local shops.
- Write a press release, and send it to your local paper.
- Get your friends to spread the word to help you out.
- Start a business Web site or get a company MySpace page. It'll help spread the word, and you can build a mailing list of interested people.

There are a ton of opportunities out there for you, so stay true to yourself and your passion, and don't settle for less. Do whatever it takes (okay, within reason) to make your dreams a reality.

Gal to Gal

"I triple-love beads! I could bead all day long, every day. I started when I was little, and it's safe to say, I'm hooked! I stared making jewelry for me and my friends, and more and more people started wanting it. Now, I sell it online, and I donate some to charity as well. So, my advice for every girl is to find what she would do for free, and turn it into a way to make money, like I did."
— Heidi, 22

"Go for it, no matter what. It took me a little longer to learn that than I would have liked, but I'm glad I learned it."
— Jill, 23

"If you hate your job, quit. Life is too short; find something that you actually like to do."
— Karen, 17

"Do something nice for your fellow employees every week. I bring in homemade cookies or cupcakes every Friday. It's not a big deal for me to do, but it means a lot to everybody, and the boss, too!"
— McKayla, 19

"If you are excited, act excited. That energy keeps everybody else going."
— Amy, 17

Hey, it's okay to:

- Change what you think you want to do a million times. Who hasn't wanted to be a doctor, vet, acrobat, author, artist, and cake baker in the span of a couple weeks?
- Change jobs and careers until you find one that suits you the best.
- Be freaked out and overwhelmed—we all are!
- Be ambitious and have really big goals; nobody is stopping you but yourself!

- Stay tuned to for a total health makeover. From your diet to your exercise regime, it's time to "Move that bus!" as Ty Pennington says. And by that I mean, "Move your behind!" because it's time to get it in gear! In a fun way, of course!

Lesson 8:
Healthy Gal 101

Who doesn't want to feel healthy, have a ton of energy, feel great about herself, and look amazing and glowing? So, why do we eat junk? What makes us sit down, frozen, in front of the TV for hours on end? Why would we rather cuddle a poisonous snake than eat a vegetable? Not only does eating right make our brains super-powerful, but it also makes our bodies super-hero strong, too. And the coolest part is that being a healthy gal is actually kind of fun. No tofu binges, marathon workout sessions, or weird contraptions required. It's all about practical ways to eat right, make healthy choices, and learn what's good and what's not good for you. It's also about knowing what stuff to avoid and how to bust stress, keep your mind healthy, and avoid addictions (and kick their scrawny little butts).

"Every human being is the author of [her] own health."
—Buddha (560–480 BC)

Being a healthy gal is not just about weight; in fact, your weight is a really small part of it. Sure, there are charts and calculations that supposedly tell you how much you should weigh, but they don't take things into consideration like your bone density, ethnicity, or muscle tone. So, let's not worry about your weight here; let's just focus on feeling amazing instead. Being healthy is about shining from the inside out because you feel so good, alive, and full of energy. By doing good stuff for your body, you will naturally find the size that is healthiest for you.

And, as always, it's up to you. But before you make your decision, check out some of the benefits of being a healthy gal.

You will:
• Have energy all day long.
• Maintain a healthy body weight.
• Give yourself "brain food" so you can focus better at school.
• Provide your body with the nutrients and vitamins it needs to stay healthy throughout your life.

If you are unhealthy, you'll feel:
• Slow, sluggish, and unmotivated.
• Drained and sleepy throughout the day.
• Tired at school and unable to concentrate.
• Cranky, moody, and bummed.

See why it's so important? But, before we dive right in and give you a mega-health makeover—you guessed it: a little checkup first!

What's Your Healthy Gal IQ?

1 = No way; **2** = Sorta, sometimes; **3** = Sure do!

1. I understand what being healthy is all about.	1	2	3
2. I enjoy eating fruits and vegetables.	1	2	3
3. I take care of my body by exercising often.	1	2	3
4. I don't drink, smoke, or do drugs.	1	2	3
5. I make healthy choices when it comes to food.	1	2	3
6. I know about the foods that my body needs.	1	2	3
7. I take the stairs, and walk or ride my bike when I can.	1	2	3
8. I know the benefits of being a Healthy Gal.	1	2	3
9. I enjoy taking care of my body.	1	2	3
10. I feel really good when I eat right or exercise.	1	2	3

Now add up the numbers and find your Healthy Gal IQ. **Total:**_____

Scoring:

10-15: All right, so you may or may not have ever eaten a vegetable, but it doesn't mean all hope is lost. You have to start somewhere, right? In fact, this is the perfect time for you to start living a healthier life—it's easier to start now than it will be for you when you're in your thirties.

16-22: Hovering right here in the middle means you're aware of how to keep healthy, but you might not always follow through. Time to step it up a notch by making some healthy (and easy) switches, and doing some awesome exercise to get you on the healthy high road!

23-30: Kudos to you, Healthy Gal! Still, it's important to make sure you are doing all that you can to be as healthy as you need to be. Learning some new tips and fun ideas for staying healthy is always a good idea.

Living a healthy life doesn't have to be hard or unsatisfying. You can still watch TV and eat all your favorite foods—in moderation. In "The Picture of Health," you'll discover what is and isn't healthy, why that's important, and what being healthy looks like. Then, in "Hungry Gal," you'll learn what kind of food you need to fuel your body and keep it going strong, along with fun ways to get it. "Gals in Motion" covers the importance of exercise and some cool and easy ways to get what you need. The last section, "Minding Your Mental Health," is dedicated to your inner health, and what you can do to keep your mind happy and healthy by managing stress, getting enough zzz's, and staying addiction-free.

The Picture of Health

"The problem with quick and convenient food is that it's usually really bad for you. I've got a really hectic schedule. so I usually just grab what's easy. but it bothers me that it's not good for me."
—Kristin, 16

"My mom is a health nut. If it were up to her. I seriously would eat just like my pet guinea pig! But I have a really good understanding of what is healthy and what isn't. and even though I don't stick to it as [strictly] as she does. I'm way healthier than most of my friends."
—Carla, 17

"I come from a family who is mostly overweight. and I've inherited the big-girl genes. also. Sometimes I feel like its unfair. but other times. I guess I think there must be something I can do about it."
—Amerie, 15

The way I see it, you have a choice. You can either eat right and exercise, or you can eat junk, smoke, drink, do drugs, have risky sexual encounters, and spend your life on the couch. You can either be healthy, or you can be unhealthy and do long-term damage to your body, your mind, and your future. (Sorry. That was a little "Dr. Phil Boot Camp-ish. Moving on …)

Just like every other part of your life, you are responsible for your health. Nobody is going to care if you don't eat right, bail on your exercise routine, start smoking, don't get your yearly ob-gyn exam, or don't take care of your mental health. Of course, your family and friends will be there for you, but it's not their responsibility. And once you hit eighteen, baby, you are on your own, so taking care of your health should start now. The sooner you start making healthy changes to your routine, the easier it will be, and the less long-term damage you will do to your bod and mind.

Your body really is a temple. That's a cliché, I know, but you are a goddess, and your body is housing your awesome self. So, by treating it right and giving it what it needs—and keeping it away from things it doesn't—you are doing your part to ensure a healthy, productive life. But what makes up a healthy life, anyway?

Components of a Healthy Life

Eating right. This means getting the right balance of energy and nutrients that your body and your mind need to function properly every day. If you get too much, you gain weight. If you get too little, you lose weight, and your body might not be able to develop at the rate it should.

Exercise. Getting your body in gear and moving does wonders for you, both physically and mentally. You gain muscle and become stronger, burn fat and calories, have endurance, and keep your heart strong. And the chemicals that exercising releases, called endorphins, make you feel super-happy.

Mental health. Managing your stress levels, getting enough sleep. and venting your emotions in a healthy way help keep your mind healthy, just like avoiding drugs and alcohol.

Recognizing Health

It can be tough to discern what's healthy and what's not, especially because we live in a society that cares more about looks than health. Any of you who have read a fashion magazine know how confusing the images in it can be. Hello? They fill the pages with scary-thin girls, looking all glowing and happy, and then include a well-meaning article on loving your body no matter its size. And then, they slap a diet ad on the next page! No wonder we are confused about what is healthy! See if you can spot the healthy gal in the examples below. (Hint: It's not the one the media would have you believe.)

Girl A: She's heavyset with curves, boobs, and booty. Her clothes are a size 12. She works out five times a week and is toned and fit. She eats a healthy diet of fruit, veggies, and the occasional chocolate bar. She doesn't smoke or drink, takes a daily multivitamin, and has a healthy body image.

Girl B: She is the "it" girl in all the magazines, weighing in at ninety-seven pounds and slipping into a size 0. She drinks, smokes, and survives on fast food and unhealthy snacks. Her idea of exercise is strutting from the salon to her SUV.

It doesn't take somebody with a PhD to tell us that Gal 1 is way up there on the healthy scale, even though Gal 2 is the one we often strive to be like. Being healthy is all about how you feel, inside and out. No matter your size or body type, the healthiest thing you can do for yourself is love who you are, and do stuff your body will love you for.

Think about it—you don't feed the people you love garbage, because it would hurt them. Same for you. Your body rocks, and even if you are still struggling to accept it, it's all you've got. So suck it up, see the big picture, and make the choice to live like a healthy gal from this point on.

Get Healthy Goal-Setting

Just because you make a goal and want it really bad doesn't mean that it is necessarily easy. If you are anything like me, you think that you'll step off the treadmill with the endurance of a triathlete and the abs of a Miss World contestant. I'm still waiting, and I've been on the treadmill three or four times, easy. (Just kidding.)

The point I think I'm trying to make is that if you set a vague goal like "getting healthy" and expect the best right way, you will be discouraged and disappointed and might fall short of reaching it. Instead, set a measurable, specific goal that you are accountable for reaching. Here's how:

1. Be specific. Which of these is a better goal? "I want to lose weight," or "I want to have more energy and fit into my old jeans by Monday, June 23"? The specific and measurable goal is the better one.

2. Be realistic! You probably know your body, and you know what kind of motivation you have, so take that into account. Remember, this isn't an overnight thing. Wanting to drop a ton of weight and look like a supermodel isn't a realistic goal for anyone! Instead, focus on what is right for you, like toning up and gaining endurance. For example, tell yourself that you'll be able to run around the track two times by the end of the school year. Or that you'll cut your soda pop intake in half by this time next month. See the difference?

3. Pick a goal that you want to reach, and do it for you, nobody else.

Use the space below to write down your "Get Healthy" goal:

_____

_____

_____

_____

_____

_____

_____

Now, close your eyes, and see yourself having reached that goal. Feel what it's like. Notice how you look, how good you feel, and even what you are wearing. Now, write your goal down again, this time on a piece of paper that you can tape to your bathroom mirror or carry in your pocket. You'll be reminded of your goal and motivated to do the work it takes to get there, each time you read it.

Now that your goal is set and you're motivated to whip yourself into a health frenzy, check out the following tips on eating like a healthy gal, followed by exercising like a star, and avoiding the really unhealthy druggy and alcoholly things.

Hungry Gal

Here's the thing about eating right: You wouldn't fill your car up with Kool-Aid, right? You'd fill it up with gasoline. Even though Kool-Aid is way cheaper than gas, you know your car wouldn't move in inch with it, and it would probably do a ton of damage to the engine. The same thing happens to your body if you eat junk.

Eating right is pretty easy, and you don't have to swear off meat, eat green stuff all day, or choke down steamed tofu every night. That's no fun. I consider myself to be healthy, even though, as I write this, I'm eating a DQ Dilly Bar. I enjoy life, and food is a huge part of that enjoyment for me. I love to cook, love to eat out at really nice restaurants, and love to try new things. But I do try to cut back on sugar whenever I can. I opt for the fat-free versions of things. And I eat lots of fruits and veggies, and choose lean meat, like chicken and fish. If I want an ice cream, a chocolate bar, or the occasional bag of chips, I have them. Everything in moderation.

Empowered Gals know that it's not just about how you look but how you feel and how well you take care of your body. Eating good things makes you feel good! But what are good things, anyway? I mean cheeseburgers taste good, right? The Dietary Guidelines for Americans describes a healthy diet as "emphasizing fruit, vegetables, whole grains, [and] fat-free or low-fat milk products. [It] includes lean meats such as poultry and fish, as well as beans, eggs, and nuts, and is low in saturated fats, trans fats, cholesterol, salt, and added sugar." Do-able right? You just need to keep an open mind and try new things. If you've had a lifelong hatred for asparagus, that's totally fine. Maybe you genuinely don't like the taste or texture, or maybe you haven't had it prepared in a way you like. Just be open to experiment a little, and find things you do like. Here are some good foods or food groups that are important for your health and ways to enjoy eating them! (Hint: fresh fruit is usually way yummier than canned or even frozen fruit, so before you skip it, try the fresh versions. Same for veggies!) For more info on healthy eating, visit www.MyPyramid.gov, where most of this info came from.

Fruity Things

These little vitamin- and nutrient-packed bad boys give you energy and fiber, and make you feel fuller than a bag of chips. Don't like fruit or veggies? Don't believe you. There are tons of different kinds, so you are bound to find a couple you "heart," and because gals between the ages of fourteen and eighteen need about 1½ cups of fruit a day, you better get experimenting!

Yummy fruits include apples, oranges, bananas, grapefruits, strawberries, raspberries, blueberries, pomegranates, passion fruit, apricots, kiwis, pears, peaches, mangos, watermelons, cantaloupes, cherries, star fruit, lychee, pineapple, tangerines, raisins, plums, lemons and limes, and avocados—to name only a few!

Not only is fruit super-yummy, but according to MyPyramid.com, the healthy-food site produced by the U.S. Dept. of Health, eating a balanced diet that includes lots of fruits and veggies will help you reduce your risk of stroke, cardiovascular and heart disease, type 2 diabetes. And it will protect against certain cancers, give you energy, and make you feel great! Plus, lots of fruits and veggies contain antioxidants, which make your skin glow!

Veggie Things

Veggies are packed full of vitamins and nutrients, are full of fiber, and can taste really good. And the good news is, you can drink your veggies too—tomato juice, for example, is delicious.

Yummy veggies include cucumbers, bell peppers, carrots, tomatoes, celery, bok choy, broccoli, collard greens, kale, lettuce, watercress, corn, peas, lima beans, potatoes, squash, pumpkin, sweet potato, beans, lentils, tofu, artichokes, asparagus, beets, bean sprouts, cauliflower, eggplant, mushrooms, parsnips, tomato juice, vegetable juice, turnips, and zucchini.

MyPyramid.gov recommends that girls between the ages of fourteen and eighteen get about 2½ cups of veggies a day. That's so do-able! And since most veggies are low in fat and calories, and none has cholesterol, you will be doing your body a mega-favor. Plus, they are important sources of potassium (which helps maintain healthy blood pressure), fiber (lowers blood cholesterol levels and lowers your risk of heart disease; plus, makes you feel fuller longer), folate (helps you form red blood cells), and vitamins A, C and E (keeps your eyes and skin healthy, protect against infections, heal cuts and wounds, and keeps gums and teeth healthy).

Grainy Things

You remember a couple years ago when everybody thought carbohydrates were the devil, and we had a ton of super-skinny cranky women running around? Yeah, I tried the no-carb thing, too. It lasted until lunch the next day, when I just about murdered my sister for her bowl of mac and cheese. It's not a good look, ladies, and carbs are pretty important little puppies when it comes to a healthy diet. They come in the form of breads, cereals, pastas, rice, and even couscous (a sort of Middle Eastern pasta—its yummy!). Try to eat the whole-grain versions when you can, like whole-grain bread, cereal, and pasta. And, just so ya know, MyPyramid.gov suggests that gals between the ages of fourteen and eighteen get about six ounces of grains a day. What's an ounce of grains, you ask? Well, generally speaking, 1 cup of cereal, 1 slice of bread, or ½ cup of cooked rice or pasta equals one ounce.

Other Important-y Things

Milk: It is recommended that you get three cups of milk a day. A cup could mean 1½ ounces of cheese, two ounces of processed cheese, or a cup of milk or yogurt. Milk helps you build strong bones, reduces the risk of osteoporosis, and maintains bone mass, especially when you are growing, which you are doing right now. Plus, it's filled with calcium, potassium, and vitamins A, D, and E, which your bones and teeth kind of love. A lot.

Protein: This includes meat, poultry, fish, beans, peas, eggs, nuts, and seeds. According to our pals at MyPyramid.com, you should be getting about five ounces a day of protein. Stuff that is considered an ounce is an egg, one tablespoon of peanut butter, ¼ cup of beans, or an ounce of meat. Why should you eat protein, you ask? Well, it's full of the really important B vitamins, vitamin E, iron (which is super-important for teen gals, who are usually lacking it), and magnesium, and it is a building block for enzymes, hormones, and vitamins. Sounds pretty good, but you do have to look out for a couple things. Some meats are high in saturated fats and cholesterol, so choose lean meats, like chicken and fish.

Essential Fatty Acids: Girls are supposed to get five tablespoons of good fats, which are often found in fish, nuts, cooking oil, and salad dressings. Always opt for polyunsaturated fats or monounsaturated fats, instead of the animal fat like you find in butters, beef, chicken or pork fat, margarine, or shortening.

So, now that you are a healthy-food expert, no more excuses! Eating healthy is fun (especially if your get your friends and family involved), nutritious, and can be really yummy, so make the effort to eat right. Ask your mom to look for the health-check symbol (it's a little green box with a checkmark) on foods at the grocery store for help in making healthy choices. Your body and your brain will thank you!

For yummy recipe ideas and tips on preparing healthy food for you, your friends and your family, check out **www.empoweredgal.com**.

Top Five EG Super-Foods

Here are some of my favorite, healthy staples:

1. Pomegranate or acai juice. It's full of antioxidants that my skin loves (yours will too)!
2. Lots of green stuff, like spinach, kale, watercress, sprouts, etc. It's not easy to eat this stuff, but you need it every day, so tough up and just do it. Your body will thank you.
3. Bags or tubs of prewashed, organic lettuce leaves. What a time saver! I always have one in the fridge, so there is no excuse not to whip up a salad or add some greens to a sandwich.
4. The essential smoothie ingredients, which are low-fat vanilla yogurt, orange juice or pomegranate juice, low-fat milk, strawberries and blueberries, and a couple chocolate chips for the top. Delicious in the morning or as an after-school snack.
5. Homemade iced tea (green or black), sweetened and flavored with honey and lemon. Tastes great, and it's great for you. (I like the pomegranate- or raspberry-flavored teas, but experiment until you find what you like.)

Three Things on Our Naughty List

If these three were kids, they'd so be sent to the corner and given coal for Christmas.

Soda pop. It's the enemy. I read some stuff about Coke that freaked me out, and I'm pretty sure I'd get sued if I wrote about it here, so instead of going there, let's just talk a little bit about how bad soda pop, in general, is for you. First, though, go and measure out nine teaspoons of sugar into a jar or bowl. I'll stop writing and wait for you to come back.

Okay, I totally know you didn't go do that, so trust me—it's a lot. And it's in every single can of soda pop that you drink. Pretty gross, hey? I actually keep a little jar by the fridge so I am not tempted to drink any when it's in the house. That much sugar is super-bad for you, so stay away. Instead, I drink pomegranate juice mixed with water or sparkling water, lemon- or lime-flavored water, home-brewed iced tea sweetened with honey, or low-fat milk. My drink of choice these days happens to be vitamin water, which has its faults but is a much wiser choice than soda pop. Or, if you can't get enough of carbonated liquids, opt for the all-natural forms that come in a wide variety of flavors and can be found at most supermarkets or health-food stores.

Fast food. How many of you, like me, swear you will never have another hamburger again after whizzing through a fast-food joint and feeling really bad after? That's because you are eating crap. It's got about 0.002% nutritional value (I just made that up, but it is probably close), and it's not real food. I don't even want to know what those patties are made of. Sure, to be fair, some places are offering healthy choices and substitutions, and that's great, so if you have to eat there, go for something that at least sounds healthy. On the other hand, it might be a good idea to cut down the frequency that you get a hot meal in thirty seconds or less, and take a couple minutes to whip up something at home that is actually good for you before you head out.

Snacks. I love snacks. The packaging gets me every time. But snacking on things that are bright orange, hot pink, or animal-shaped might not always be your best choice. I hate to break it to you, but Cheetos don't grow on trees. Snacks are super-important throughout the day, and you need them to keep your energy level up. But by choosing ones out the vending machine, you aren't doing yourself any favors. Instead, pack some of the following into your lunch bag: cheese and crackers, veggies and dip, strawberries and chocolate sauce, unsalted and unbuttered popcorn, tortilla chips and salsa, carrots and hummus, hard-boiled eggs, cheese-stuffed celery sticks, or pretzels. It's a good thing, as Martha Stewart would say. You deserve the best in every area of your life; your food should be no different!

On a side note here, you've heard me mention that you need to make your life work for you. I guess, with my background in business and growing up around my dad's running his business, I expect everything in my life to work for me. My diet needs to work for me, my friendships need to work for me, my relationships need to work for me, and on and on. If my food is making me feel bad, causing me to lose energy, and keeps me up all night, I'm gonna fire it and find a replacement, no questions asked. Be the boss in your own life, and cut out what doesn't work for you.

Smart Tricks: Minding Your Meals and Munchies Ahead of Time

I get that it can be hard, as a teen, to always eat right. After all, you are always on the go and aren't necessarily responsible for the kind of food that comes into your house. But that shouldn't be an excuse, so here are some snazzy little tips on eating right—and you do control here.

- When you eat out, order an appetizer as a main meal, or order half a portion instead of the entire plate of fettuccini Alfredo. It's no secret that restaurant-sized portions are crazy big. Plus, try to leave some leftovers to take home.
- Don't snack straight from the bag when you are in the middle of a My Super Sweet 16 marathon! Instead, take one serving, and put it in a bowl or cup, and leave the bag in the cupboard—where it belongs! This will save mindless snacking and a belly full of empty calories.
- Slow down and take the time to enjoy what you are eating. It'll last longer, and you'll feel fuller, sooner, so you won't overeat.
- Go online on the weekend, pick some healthy recipes, and cook them with a pal. Pop them in the freezer, and thaw throughout the week for quick, healthy, convenient meals.

Making Healthy Switches

Remember, eating healthy doesn't mean eating like a rabbit, surviving on tofu and sprouts, or changing your name to Willow. It's easy, it's worth it, and you can totally do it. Here are some healthy switches you can start making today. Switch:
- Chips and dip for pitas and hummus

- Soda pop for homemade iced tea
- Ice cream for frozen yogurt
- Whole-fat dairy for low-fat dairy
- Candy for sugar-free sweets or dried fruit

Easy ways to save calories each day include:

- Eat breakfast. You won't feel like grabbing unhealthy snacks if you fill up on protein in the morning.
- Opt for the sugar-free or fat-free versions of your fave foods.
- Choose the healthy selections from the menu or cafeteria.
- Drink one glass of water before a meal, so you'll feel fuller sooner.
- Use vinaigrettes instead of creamy salad dressings or dips.
- Make your own snacks before school, instead of buying them from vending machines.
- Use mustard instead of fatty mayo on your sandwiches.

EG Tip: Educate yourself. Search the Internet for healthy recipes and ways to cook things. The more you know about food and your choices, the more likely you are to eat healthfully throughout your life.

Be a Better Eater

- Learn to cook for yourself and your family.
- Start suggesting healthy alternatives or recipes for your entire family.
- Don't eat on the run. It always bugs me when I cook dinner, and people just stand over the counter, eating it. Sit down and enjoy it!
- Buy food in season (strawberries in the spring; squash in the fall). It tastes great and is usually cheaper.
- Eat because you are hungry, not because you are bored or looking for comfort. Try volunteering or getting an after-school job to help keep you busy and feel better about yourself, so you don't look to food to do that for you.
- Sit down with your family and eat together. Talk about your day.
- Try new stuff. Did you see something at the supermarket you've never seen before? Buy it, and give it a try!
- Plan your meals ahead of time. If you have healthy ingredients on hand and know what snacks you want to take to school with you, you'll be way less likely to space out on junk or rob the vending machine of all its Doritos.

- Educate your family. They may not know the importance of eating healthfully, so show them this chapter, and see if you can all work together to be healthier.
- Go to www.empoweredgal.com and download the healthy shopping lists. You can stick them on your fridge, and tick off when you are running low. It'll help your mom out, too!

Are you surprised that making little changes can really make a difference? It's not hard to eat healthfully, and now, more than ever, there are lots of healthy options and choices all around you.

Now that I have you all fueled up on nutrients, vitamins, and stuff you body will thank you for, let's move onto getting your booty-licious behind in gear!

Gals in Motion

"I don't 'exercise' like most people think of exercising. I play volleyball, walk to the baby-sitters to pick up my little sister after school, ride my bike to the store or to see my friends. I help my dad around the yard, and I give my all in gym class! Exercising doesn't mean hitting the gym for an hour a day; you can easily incorporate it into your life. It's just a choice."
—Roberta, 17

"My friends and I are really active. We play sports, go to the gym. We head to the park to play football with the guys. we rollerblade along the beach, and we get the most of what California has to offer!"
—Georgia, 17

Just as eating the right food is important to living a healthy, well-balanced life, so is exercise. Before you jump to any conclusions about exercise or come up with super-lame but convincing excuses for not doing it, let me tell you what it does for you:
- It helps you stay a healthy weight, builds muscle, and improves your endurance.
- It reduces your risk for heart disease, high blood pressure, high cholesterol, and diabetes later in life. If you start now, it will be easier than starting fifteen years from now.
- It helps your flexibility and balance.

- It improves your outlook on life, as well as your mood, body image, and confidence.
- It helps you de-stress and re-energize your body and your mind.

Next time you are zoning out in front of your computer, think about what just thirty minutes of exercise will do for you. Plus, it doesn't have to be super-rigorous, exhausting, boring, terrifying, confusing, or whatever else pops into your mind when you think of it. It can be fun, and it's sometimes just a matter of spreading it out throughout your day by being a little creative. You will feel energized, invigorated, and feel way more positive, thanks to those darling little endorphins!

Fun Ways to Stay Healthy

Yes, you read that right. Getting the recommended amount of physical activity can be fun!

- Ride your bike to school, around the block, or to your friend's house instead of being driven.
- Join a sports team. It doesn't even matter if you are any good—well, it might to your team—just get out there and have fun! If it feels fun, it won't feel like work, and you'll actually do it.
- Take dance classes. And by classes I mean weekly meetings with a dance teacher, although it also works to turn up your iPod and dance around your room like a mad woman. Either way …
- Hike, jog, or go for walks. Take your dog or ferret, and pound the pavement.
- Go swimming. It's low impact, and you build a ton of core strength. Plus, Marco Polo, anyone?
- Volunteer for something active, like Habitat for Humanity, or clean up the neighborhood park.
- Have a made-up tournament with some pals, where you compete by playing badminton, road hockey, or bike racing for a trophy that you pass back and forth with each win.
- Try a bunch of different stuff. You might not "hit it off" with a sports team, but you may find you really love taking long walks or doing yoga with your friends three times a week. Find what works for you.

"My friends and I wanted to start working out, so we made a pact to do it together at least three times a week. The penalty for missing out was ten dollars, and when you are a college student, that's Friday

174

night entertainment! So, in the beginning, there were a couple slip-ups, but after a while, we all stuck with it. We felt great!"

—Laura, 21

Sneaky Ways to "Work Out"

Who wants to be gym rat? If you ask me, the gym is the worst place to go to get in shape if you are just starting out, especially in L.A. I made that mistake! Everybody was so blonde, golden, and skinny that I felt like some mutant kind of beached Canadian whale. Instead, I went for walks on the beach, jogged around the block, and fit some uber-sneaky moves into my daily routine. You can, too:

- Take the stairs instead of the elevator.
- Get a tachometer. You know, those cute little puppies you stick on your belt that measure the number of steps you take every day? Challenge yourself to take more and more steps every day.
- Take a walk with your friends around the sports field at your school during lunch, instead of gabbing in the cafeteria.
- Steal a tennis ball from your dog, and play catch with your friends while you wait for the bus.
- Get a group of pals together and meet in the gym at school for early-bird yoga.
- Kids down the street playing street hockey or soccer? Join in for a bit.
- Hop off the bus, or ask your ride to drop you off a couple blocks before or after your house, and walk the rest of the way.
- Shop! Yup, all that walking counts for something!

Exercise For Your Mood

Different kinds of physical activity have different kinds of benefits, from stress reduction to anger management. Check out the perfect exercise for your mood, below:

If you are super stressed try thirty minutes of yoga or Pilates, followed by ten to fifteen minutes of meditation.

If you want to improve your sportsmanship or team spirit, try soccer, basketball, or baseball.

If you want to take out your anger, try boxing, kick-boxing, or karate.

If you want to sculpt your muscles, try hitting the gym, weight lifting, or doing push-ups or sit-ups.

If you want to burn some energy, try dancing, aerobics, cycling, jogging, or power walking.

EG Tip: So what if you are unfit, feel like you look reee-diculous in Spandex workout gear, or think that you jiggle way too much when you run! You have to start somewhere, so swallow your pride, give yourself a mega-dose of affirmations, and head out! You will be glad you did—and will be slightly less and less jiggly each time you do it.

Minding Your Mental Health

"Sometimes. I get really depressed and down. Life just seems so hard sometimes. and I can't wait for it to get better."
—Rosa, 15

"I try to be positive. but sometimes the stress gets to me. I'm not going to lie. It's hard to cope with all the pressure. and sometimes I just feel like crawling in a hole until it gets better. But the good thing is. it always does get better."
—Anita, 18

Just as you need to take care of your physical health by eating right and shakin' what your mamma gave ya, you also need to take care of your mental health—that means how you feel about yourself, life, and the world around you. If you don't, you could end up feeling depressed, tired, sad, or down, or even do stuff to harm yourself, like cutting yourself or doing drugs. Your mood and mental health are affected by lots of things, including hormones, brain chemicals, traumatic stuff happening in your family, good or bad times with your friends, fights, what kind of food you eat, how much sleep you get, stress, and how much activity you get.

You have control over some of those things, and some you don't. But there is stuff you can do to feel like your good old self, even if you are still trying to figure out who that is. Just remember that this is a really big, complicated subject, so I'm just going to go over some basic stuff here. You'll need to consult your doctor for more detailed info that applies to you. Use this as a starting off point.

Hey, it's normal to feel:

Sad, confused, down, unhappy, cranky, like crying (over really small things), worried, stressed (over everything from pimples to the state of the economy), mad, angry, emotional, perplexed, like you are on a roller coaster, or scared

But if you feel these things all the time, and they are beginning to take over your life, talk to somebody about it. There is zero shame in getting help and doing whatever it takes to feel good again. Life is way too short and amazing to spend it wrapped up in a blanket, rocking back and forth in your room. There are people who went to school for a really, really long time and have a whole lot of experience who know exactly what you are going through and how to help you. If you are feeling depressed, if you have suicidal thoughts or an eating disorder, if you do harmful stuff to yourself, or even if you are just tired of crying all the time, talk to a professional. You will be glad you did (and so will I).

You can talk to your parents, teachers, or relatives first, and they will probably suggest that you go to see your family doc, who will then refer you to a counselor or therapist who will be best suited to help you.

How to Keep Feeling Great

- Have people you can talk to about big and little things. Sometimes just getting stuff off your chest lets you clear your head and feel better.
- Fill up on healthy foods and "brain foods," like blueberries, nuts, and fish (a good source of omega-3 fatty acids). They keep your brain working hard.
- Get enough sleep.
- Surround yourself with supportive, loving people.
- Have a mood-boosting playlist that you can put on to cheer yourself up.
- Learn how to manage your stress.
- Stay active. It improves your mood like you wouldn't believe.

Staving Off Moodiness with Adequate Sleep

I don't know about you, but I love being in bed. I love it—it's so cozy, and I have about a million pillows and quilts and, of course, little Allie in there with me. It's my favorite place. Maybe it's because I travel so much, but I believe Dorothy almost had it right: there is no place like home. There is certainly no place like your own bed. I like to go to bed early and wake up early. Or not. Sometimes I like to sleep in, but I'm trying to make a point. Whenever I stay up past midnight, I feel really groggy and foggy the next day, and—dare I say it?—a little cranky, too. Play around with your bedtime to see how you feel.

Speaking of sleeping in, it's not a good idea to break the pattern too much. I remember in high school how I'd get up at six o'clock every day during the week and sleep until about 10:30 on the weekends. I later found out that it's not a good idea to switch things up too much. Try to stay consistent with your bedtime and wake-up hours. Experts suggest no more that two hours difference on either side.

Research shows that a lack of sleep leads to:

• Depression

• Moodiness

• Poor school performance

• Emotional distress

• Accidents and injuries

You know what it's like; we've all been there. You stay up surfing perezhilton.com, and before you know it, it's 2 AM. If you have to get up early the next day, you can be irritable, moody, snap at the smallest things, and let small issues get completely out of control. Lack of sleep makes things seem overwhelming. Your concentration goes out the window, and even the most patient friends don't want to be around you.

Most teen girls get between six and eight hours of sleep, on average, but sleep researchers suggest that teens should get between 8½ and 9½ hours each night. So, plan ahead. To help with your planning, fill out the following chart:

In order to get _____ hours of sleep and be up by _____ AM, I need to go to bed by _____ PM.

Falling Asleep

It usually takes me about an hour to fall asleep. I've got so much on my mind that I just can't seem to chill out. I know it's the same for a lot of you, so here's what I recommend:

Take a bath. Put some vanilla and lavender bath oil in the tub and just relax with the lights dimmed for about ten or fifteen minutes. It'll help you to de-stress. You could even listen to some relaxing tunes while you are at it.

Aromatherapy. Fill a spray bottle with lavender and water, and spray your pillow, or tuck a potpourri pouch of lavender by your bed. It'll help you relax and doze off.

Have some milk. I can't prove it, but I'm sure milk before bed helps me fall asleep quicker! Plus, avoid caffeine (coffee, dark chocolate, tea, or soda pop) for four to six hours before bed.

Journal. This is one of my favorite things to do before bed. I love to write in my journal. You can either write about your day, stuff that's on your mind or worrying you, important stuff you don't want to forget, or a to-do list for tomorrow. No matter what I write about, I always wrap it up with writing about what I'm most grateful for.

Use your bed for sleeping only. It can be super-tempting to study in your bed or do your homework while tucked in, but it's important for your bed to be just for sleeping. If you are used to working in it, you'll be less able to unwind and fall asleep in it.

Combating Stress

You can be a (relatively) stress-free gal. Sure, there are stresses that we just can't control, like a sick parent, an accident, or bad news from a friend or a relative. But I'm talking about the daily stress, like homework, friends, school, parents, etc. It's that stuff that really takes a toll, because there is no escape from it. But if you get all those things filed away in their proper place and find balance, you will be able to deal with the stress a whole lot better. And let's face it: who doesn't want to be stress-free?

Stress-Busting Tips

- Write it down. Instead of running around, trying to remember every little detail of every little thing you have to do, take a load off and just write it down. You'll rest a lot easier, knowing that it's all safely on paper and not racing through your mind!

- Deal with it. Worried about what's going on with your parents? Not sure why your boyfriend is acting weird? Can't figure out why your friend suddenly stopped talking to you? Deal with it by going to the source of your stress and finding out what's really going on. The chances are that it's not as bad as you think, and it'll be one less thing on your mind.

- Have chill time. There is no law that says you need to fill your schedule up to the brim. Instead, take a bubble bath, light candles, watch your favorite episodes of your favorite shows, write poetry, decorate your room, paint, draw, listen to music, read a book, or go to the park. Whatever it is, give yourself permission to take a little time off.

- Set limits. If you are constantly tied to your computer, cell phone, or PDA, you, like it, are never "off." Start by turning your cell phone and computer off for an hour a day. Be unreachable. You won't miss anything important; trust me. To prove my point, go back over all the e-mails and texts you received in the last hour. I'll bet you no one mentioned anything about the impending Apocalypse. And if anything life-changing did occur in your hour of bliss, I'm sure somebody will find another way to tell you. Anything else can wait.

Coping with Depression

I have never met girl who, at some point, hasn't felt depressed. It's no wonder, with all the changes you are going through right now! Hormones, stress, pressure, traumatic events, disasters, divorce, breakups, and those mean girls we talked about earlier can all contribute to feeling depressed. But there is a difference between feeling down once in a while and having full-on depression.

Symptoms of Depression
- Feeling sad and crying without necessarily knowing why
- Eating way less or way more than usual
- Having super-low confidence or self-esteem, even though you have a lot going for you
- Withdrawing from your friends
- Not doing your regular activities or losing interest in them
- Feeling tired all the time and possibly sleeping more, or having trouble sleeping at all

- Feeling negative about everything
- Feeling irritated, moody, crabby, and anxious
- Not being able to focus, especially at school
- Losing interest in things you used to love
- Thinking about death or even suicide

We all feel some of these things from time to time, but if you experience more than one, and have for a few weeks, you might be depressed.

Here's what you can do if you are feeling down or sad:
- Talk to your mom or dad, teachers, friends, or school nurse or counselor.
- Make an appointment with your family doctor, and ask about your options.
- Start exercising. When you exercise, you release endorphins that make you feel better; plus, it will help you de-stress and reflect.
- Read uplifting or inspiring books or stories. (Stock up on Chicken Soup for the Soul.)
- Listen to your favorite uplifting music.
- Make an effort to go out and do the things you used to love, even if you don't feel like it.
- Get out of your head for a while and go to help somebody. It doesn't even matter what you are doing. You could volunteer at a retirement home, or walk dogs at your local shelter. Helping somebody else feel better will make you feel a whole lot better, too; I guarantee it.

No matter what it is, how bad you are feeling, or how sure you are things will never get better, know that if you have a pulse, you have a purpose, and things will one day get better. It's hard, and it sucks, and you might even be crying right now. I know how you feel. I used to be depressed, too. If that is you right now, cry a little longer, but then listen to that voice inside you, telling you that tomorrow will be better. Keep on going until you get there.

Eating Disorders

The National Institute of Mental Health estimates that one in five girls will experience some form of an eating disorder in their lifetimes. If you are one of those girls, remember that you are way too fabulous to be harming yourself and feeling that way. Don't worry if you can't get a handle on it on your own; having an eating disorder isn't just about trying to lose weight. It's a psychological illness, and it's not your fault.

Remember, there is no shame or weakness in admitting you need help. In fact, it takes somebody super-strong to admit she can't do it alone. If you aren't sure if you have a problem—or if you're wondering if one of your gal pals does—here are some of the things to look for.

- Loss of a lot of weight
- Prolonged dieting
- Feeling fat all the time
- Being obsessed with food, eating, and calories
- A fear of gaining weight
- Secretive eating patterns
- Not wanting anybody to eat in front of others
- Not wanting to discuss food, diet, or exercise
- Exercising for prolonged periods of time
- Eating when you aren't hungry
- Looking for comfort, support, or love in food and overeating
- Binge eating
- Weighing yourself once or more every day
- Making up excuses about your weight, food intake, or exercise
- Depression, low self-esteem, and poor body image
- Throwing up after eating, even only once in a while
- Feeling weak and exhausted often
- Mood swings
- Feeling out of control
- Irregular periods, or loss of your menstrual cycle altogether
- Hair loss

If you can relate to these feelings or symptoms, whether you are underweight, overweight, or somewhere in the middle, then you owe it to yourself to reach out to somebody you can trust (whether just one person or a support group), so that you can get better. For more information go to www.edap.org.

Angry Gals

It's too bad that some girls think they can't get emotional or show anger. Instead, they bottle it up until one day it erupts, like Mt. Vesuvius, and they end up the star of their very own YouTube video, pummeling a girl in the school cafeteria. So, here's a little secret I'm gonna let you in on: Anger is a natural, totally okay emotion to have. It's even okay to express it. I know ... crazy, right?

Guys are always praised for their "aggression" on the football field or their "strength" when they "totally lost it on some guy." But we gals are supposed to be all ladylike when some girl does something super-shady. I think not!

Before you get all Fight Club, here are some things to remember when it comes to girl anger:

- Be honest—did the girl who accidentally bumped into you in the hallway really make you lose it, or did your outburst have something to do with your parents' fighting all the time? Usually, if we bottle up how we really feel, it comes out in totally weird ways. Take a walk and figure out what is really making you so angry and upset.
- If something really makes you mad, don't let it slide. Talk to somebody about it, whether it's a friend, teacher, parent, or that old lady you sit next to on the bus. Keeping it all locked up is not a good idea.
- If you have smoke coming out your ears, give yourself a chill-out period so you can come back down to earth. When your head is clearer, you'll be able to see the whole situation a lot better and figure out your next move, instead of acting impulsively.
- Write about it. Keeping a journal is a great way to figure yourself out and what is really bothering you. It also helps you to make sense of whatever it was that made you mad.
- If you find yourself repeating patterns that make you angry, start finding ways to avoid it. If that one girl always gets under your skin, avoid her. If your parents' fighting drives you up the wall, talk to them about it, or spend a couple nights a week at a friend's or relative's house to avoid it.
- Wait 'til you've calmed down before you confront the person who made you angry in the first place. Think about both sides, and plan out what you want to say. Let her know what you expect her to do or say to make it right. And if you did something you regret, apologize.
- Keep your hands off whoever is making you angry. Nobody wants to be splashed all over the Internet in all their tacky cell-phone-video glory or be known as Boxing Betty. If you feel like expressing your anger or emotions physically, do it in a healthy, safe way, like at the gym or taking it out on your pillow in your room.

Addictions: Avoiding, Overcoming, and Surviving

Nobody is above addictions—just look at the news. Young celebs are checking themselves into rehab every day. It's a really scary reality that addictions happen, and they can happen to anyone, even you. No matter how many times you've heard things like:

- "Everybody is doing it; it's no big deal."
- "You won't get addicted on your first try."
- "It won't hurt you—tons of kids have done it."

And no matter how many times you've told yourself:

- "I don't have an addictive personality. I'll be fine."
- "One time isn't going to hurt me. I'm not like those people."
- "I can quit any time I want. I'm totally not addicted!"

Addictions can happen, but you can avoid them altogether if you decide to play it smart, avoid situations where there are going to be drugs or alcohol, and learn to say no.

Some of the common reasons that girls drink, smoke, or do drugs is because of:

- Low self-esteem
- Peer pressure
- Family history
- Wanting to be cool
- Wanting to rebel
- Wanting to prove their independence
- Wanting to escape a painful situation
- Wanting to cope with difficult emotions

There are so many different kinds of addictions, including gambling, eating, sleeping, sex, shopping, porn, and the Internet. I am only going to cover alcohol, tobacco, and drugs here. If you are struggling with addiction, talk to an adult, and get help. Addiction can destroy your life if you don't get treatment.

The scary thing about an addiction is that it controls you. You can't ever control it, and it doesn't just affect you. Your family, friends, and teachers all have to deal with the consequences of your addiction. Plus, it is unlikely you will ever live up to your potential, become the fabulous gal you are meant to be, or reach any of your goals in life if you are constantly looking for your next fix.

Gateway Drugs

Gateway drugs include cigarettes, marijuana, and alcohol. They are called gateway drugs because they often lead (or are the "gateway") to other, more serious drugs. This often happens as you search for the high or buzz that you no longer get from your first drug choice, especially if you have an addictive personality or are going through a difficult situation.

Alcohol

Who hasn't snuck some of Mom's wine when nobody was looking or tried a sip of Dad's scotch? It's fine to be curious, but alcohol is a much bigger deal when you start drinking it. According to the National Center for Injury Prevention and Control, the three leading causes of death in young people are homicides, suicide, and car accidents, in which alcohol plays a substantial role. Alcohol is a super-deadly drug for teens and is much more of a big deal than you might think.

Alcohol affects your vision, judgment, reflexes, and vision. If you have too much, it can lead to passing out or alcohol poisoning. Plus, it'll put you at risk for being taken advantage of sexually.

Three-quarters of date rapes are related to drinking alcohol. And you can bet that all those Girls Gone Wild girls have been drinking. Why else would they do that? So, let's get real. Being drunk is not classy at all. I hate seeing girls drunk—even when they are of legal drinking age.

I'm not going to be a hypocrite, because I do drink occasionally. I've been drunk once in my life, at my dad's b-day party. It was after everybody went home, and we were all sitting outside and having fun, and I was curious. I figured I was in the safest place possible, and I had one more Cosmo than I should have. But let me tell you, that's where the fun stopped. I felt awful, I couldn't walk straight, and I couldn't stop laughing. My sister videotaped me, and I had a silver bowl on my head as I told jokes. Then, I threw up and went to bed. I'd never been drunk before that time, and so my dad and his girlfriend slept outside my room to make sure I didn't die in my sleep, which I was convinced would happen.

I can laugh about it now, but at the time, I felt so bad, and the next day I felt even worse. Now, knowing what it feels like to be wasted, I can't imagine what would have happened if I'd been younger and at a party with older guys. There is no way I could have fought off an attacker or made sensible decisions.

Alcohol makes you do stuff you wouldn't normally do. If you have your mind made up that you're not going to have sex, if you drink too much, it might not seem like such a big deal. Or, if you don't do drugs, it might not seem like such a big deal to try a hit of E, either.

Plus, you can still have fun and not drink—here's why:
- You will actually remember what you did and the fun you had.
- You don't have to worry about a drunken video of you appearing on YouTube, being taken advantage of, or getting a bad reputation.
- You won't wake up with a killer hangover and ruin the next day.
- You won't totally embarrass yourself in front of your crush.¬¬

Bottom line: Drinking irresponsibly makes you look like an idiot, and you can really easily end up doing something you regret, get taken advantage of, or worse.

Smoking

According to the World Health Organization, one in five people between ages thirteen and fifteen smoke worldwide, and eighty thousand to one hundred thousand young people start smoking every day. The scary fact is you can become addicted after your very first cigarette, and thirty-three percent of people who start smoking in their teens will eventually die of lung, mouth, throat, or another kind of cancer. It makes your teeth go yellow, your skin age, and your clothes and hair stink. It makes it hard to breathe, ruins your immune system, and can kill the people around you (from secondhand smoke).

Tobacco companies spend over one million dollars every hour on advertising, much of which is directed at young men and women. Why? They know if they get you hooked now, you'll be a lifelong customer—a life that's usually cut short by their product. And here's the thing: They never have cared about you—and never will—and they don't care about the millions of people who die each year because of their products.

Forget the ads of glamorous women with their long cigarettes. Have you ever seen a woman in real life who looks like that while smoking a cigarette? Maybe between coughs, but give me a break. The only way Big Tobacco will stop targeting young people is if you take a stand and refuse to ever give them a penny. The money you spend on cigarettes (money that you could spend on clothes, music, or a down payment on a car) is lining the pockets of people who profit from the deaths of their customers, and it's going into those ads in magazines that try to get other teens to start smoking, too.

Bottom Line: Smoking is beyond stupid, and you are way smarter, capable, and too worthy to kill yourself. If you haven't started, don't, and if you have, get help. It's not easy, but it's easier than cancer, chemo, and your parents having to bury you.

When I did an online search, I got (no kidding) 48,600,000 results for "quitting smoking." So check it out for yourself for some awesome resources to help you kick the habit.

Marijuana

Did you know that the stereotypes of the burners you see on TV, who lie around in their underwear all day, are actually true? Marijuana use has been proven to make the users less motivated and less goal-oriented. Plus, the effects on your lungs are the same as if you smoked four cigarettes—and you don't know what else you could be inhaling. It's a common practice to lace marijuana with things like cocaine and—get this—embalming fluid. Gross.

Bottom Line: If you value your goals, dreams, and future, just say no.

Other Drugs

There are too many drugs to mention, but some of the most common include Ecstasy, cocaine, heroin, Ketamine, meth, GHB, and prescription drugs including OxyContin, Percocet, and other painkillers. Sadly, these are often the drugs of choice for thousands of young women, because they think the drug will help them stay awake, have more energy, or lose weight. That kind of thinking comes at a terrible price.

Some side effects of taking these and other drugs include:
• Brain damage
• Anxiety
• Panic attacks
• Depression
• Moodiness and irritability
• Sleep problems
• Loss of interest in stuff you used to enjoy
• Pushing away the people you love
• Poor performance in school
• Likelihood of date rape increases
• Death

Listen, ladies, I know drugs are bad; you know drugs are bad. When you do them, you are giving up on your dreams, whether or not you are aware of it. A drug addict doesn't get her PhD, she doesn't get to the top of a huge corporation, and she doesn't make a good mom or wife. She ends up like every other drug addict you see.

Remember that drug addicts started out like you, but drugs don't care who you are or how sure you are that you'll be fine. They ruin lives, and I hope by now you see that you have a lot to live for! (Okay, so enough of that; I'm totally sounding like one of those terrible speakers that your school hires to tell you that "drugs are bad.")

Find Your Anti-Alcohol or Anti-Drug

For me, my "anti-alcohol/anti-drug" was my business and my dreams. I just didn't see the point of getting high with a bunch of losers when I could be working on stuff that would ultimately bring me closer to the vision I had for myself and for my life. For you, it might be your family, your little brother or sister, sports, your career, school performance, or your health. Write down your anti-drug, below.

My anti-drug is _____

Once you know what it is, it'll be way easier for you to refuse to do drugs, drink, or smoke, and you'll avoid situations in which you would be faced with those decisions.

Check out the following scenarios—you might be faced with something like this, or maybe you already have been faced with it. Figuring out how you will react in advance puts you in the driver's seat and prepares you for making the right decision. Choose the response that you feel would work best for you, below, or come up with your own answer:

Scenario # 1: Your friend Sara comes up to you at the school dance and tells you to follow her to the restroom. Once inside, you are greeted by four other friends who are all giggling. You ask what's going on, and Sara pulls out a bottle of vodka. She unscrews the top and takes a swig. She passes it to the other girls, who happily gulp it down. When it's your turn, you:
a) Say, "Sara, you know I don't drink. You guys go ahead, but you can count me out." And then you leave.
b) Tell her, "No, thanks. My parents would totally kill me, then bring me back to life, just so they could ground me till I was thirty. I better not." Then you leave.

c) Say, "No way. That's crazy. And you guys shouldn't, either. If you get caught, you'd be in so much trouble. Let's get back out there."

d) (Your answer) _____

Scenario # 2: Tim, the guy you've been crushing on for months, comes up to you one day in the hall and invites you to hang out with him at the park after school. You can't believe it, and you tell all your friends. You dash to the bathroom to fix your hair and makeup before dashing to the park to hang out. When you get there, you find him and a couple of his other hot friends with him. You walk over and notice that they are all smoking. Tim gives you a hug and offers you a cigarette. You say:

a) "Sorry, Tim, I thought you knew I didn't smoke."

b) "If I went home smelling like smoke, I'd be beyond grounded. My parents are super-strict, and they'd for sure find out. I better get out of here. If you want to hang out with me and not smoke, just let me know."

c) "And smell like an ash tray? You've got to be kidding me! Why are you smoking anyway? Why don't you put that out, and we can play a game of Frisbee?"

d) (Your answer) _____

Scenario # 3: You finally get invited to Kelsey's slumber party. It's the biggest party of the year, but it has the smallest guest list. Kids have sold invitations for hundreds of dollars, so it's kind of a big deal. Once you get there, you notice that a couple of the girls, including the Queen Bee who invited you, are doing drugs. She sees you've arrived and waves you over. Then she offers you a hit. You say:

a) "Oh, Kelsey, I thought you knew. I don't do drugs, and I'm not about to start now. I don't want to get addicted."

b) "Um, I didn't know there were going to be drugs at the party. I don't mean to sound like a party-pooper, but I'm really not comfortable with that. My mom is practically the driving force behind the anti-drug movement, and if she found out, I wouldn't see the light of day for about a month. I hope you understand."

c) "Are you serious? Kelsey, there are way better ways to have fun at a party. Why don't you put that away and get out the game of Twister?"

d) (Your answer) _____

_____

It's really easy to say no, especially if you have a strong anti-drug. Just ask yourself what's more important—graduating, or impressing some girls who don't really even care about you? And why should you poison yourself so you can hook up with a guy who is killing himself as well?

Bottom Line: There is never a right time to do drugs.

Cool Ways to Say No

- "No, thanks. Not for me."
- "Um, no way. Absolutely not. Never."
- "I'm actually working on quitting."
- "Are you kidding? My mom always smells it on my clothes (sees it in my eyes, can tell by my mood). I don't want to get busted again."
- "I'm allergic."
- "No way. I'm totally over it."
- "It actually totally affects my mood (behavior, activity level), so I'm gonna have to say no."
- "If I get caught again, I won't get to use the car for the rest of the year, so it's just not worth it."
- "My boyfriend would kill me if he found out. No thanks!"

Get the picture? There are a million ways to say no. Go ahead - get creative.

Gal to Gal

"Just make the effort, you know. It your responsibility what you put in your mouth, so eat what is good for you, and you'll feel good."
—Sara, 18

"Build a support system. It really helps that you have somebody to talk to whenever you need, whether it is for drugs, alcohol, or food."
—Jenny, 17

"Don't have junk food in the house. If it's not there, you won't be able to eat it. Ask your mom or dad to keep it out the house, and buy healthy snacks and stuff instead."
—Lisa, 18

"It's easy to give in to peer pressure if you don't have goals or plans for your life, but when you do give in and do drugs or drink, it's like you are giving up on yourself, so invest in yourself first and stand up for yourself."
—Jess, 17

Hey, it's okay to:
- Actually like things like spinach, sprouts, and tofu. I do!
- Indulge in your "weakness," like ice cream or chocolate—guilt free! Just remember, moderation is key!
- Consider that doing your hair is a workout—for some of us, it is!
- Spend some of your dough on healthy food for your family to show them that healthy can be yummy if they just give it a chance.
- Drag your mom, kicking and screaming, from the house for a morning workout. She'll thank you for it!

-Stay tuned for our final chapter on being a socially responsible gal—you know, somebody who gives back, makes a difference in the world, and helps save our beautiful planet earth by going green. No, not in a Kermit kind of way; in a planet loving kind of way. It's one of my fave topics, so see you there!

Lesson 9:

Socially Responsible Gal 101

Giving back and making a difference is the best feeling in the entire world. And the coolest part is, you can totally start making a difference right now! You don't need any kind of super-powers, tons of dough in the bank, or celebrity status to start changing the world. In fact, if you look around the house, I'm sure you can find a couple lights to switch off, which saves a ton of energy and contributes to making this world a safer, healthier place for us and for future generations. You can also get your friends together and raise money for a cause you believe in and support. Educate your peers on what they can do, get your school to start reducing its carbon emissions, and so much more! Because who doesn't want to make a difference and change the world, especially when it's so easy? (Did you know that you have already done something to make the world better? You bought this book, and a portion of the money you spent is on its way to helping a whole bunch of girls around the world. Kudos to you!)

"Think about what you have to give, not even in terms of dollars, because I believe that your life is about service. It's about what you came to give to the world, to your children, to your family."
—Oprah Winfrey

Teen girls spend billions of dollars on makeup, clothes and entertainment each year. Do you know how much money it would take to make sure every single child around the world gets an education,? Only nine to twelve billion dollars. If every kid got to go to school and got an education, they could pull themselves, their families, their communities, and then their countries out of poverty. The occurrences of HIV/AIDS would diminish; preventable diseases could be avoided; countries could build a sustainable infrastructure; and medicine, hospitals, teachers, books, clean water, human rights, and equal rights for every girl and woman would be a reality. Do you see why, maybe, if we all came together, we could totally change the world? We can do so much, and it's not even all that hard! Plus, if we all make small changes around our homes and communities, we could help our beautiful planet out of the major crisis she is in now. You and me, sistah, whadda you say? Check your IQ first, and then learn how we can do so much good together. Choose 1, 2, or 3.

What's Your Socially Responsible Gal IQ?

1 = No way; **2** = Sorta, sometimes; **3** = Sure do!

	1	2	3
1)I grew up in family that is generous with their giving.	1	2	3
2)I always help out when somebody is in need.	1	2	3
3)I love the feeling I get when I help somebody.	1	2	3
4)I love to give back, give advice, and lend a hand.	1	2	3
5)I give a percentage of my money to people in need.	1	2	3
6)I am aware of what's going on in the world.	1	2	3
7)I stay up to date on current events and topics.	1	2	3
8)I have at least one cause that is super-important to me.	1	2	3
9)I make an effort to be "green."	1	2	3
10)I do what I can to cut back on my carbon emissions.	1	2	3

Now add up the numbers and find your IQ.   **Total:** _____

Scoring:

10-15: You have a few things to learn about giving back, but you probably want to make a difference, which is a super-important start. Giving back and making a difference will change your life.

Try to do one or two small things a day, and you won't believe how great you are gonna feel.

16-22: If you fall here, you kind of know what's going on, and do your part once in a while. It's time to get inspired to make social responsibility an even bigger part of your life.

23-30: It looks like you are hooked on giving back and helping the environment. Keep making a difference!

Okay, I'm just going to say it: I love to give! I love to make a difference and do stuff to help people. And, if you don't already, you will by the end of this lesson! In "Giving Gal," you'll find out the impact you can have and the difference you can make. You'll learn the small things you can do every day, and the stuff you can do to literally change the world. (It's way easier than you think!) In "Green Gal," you will find your polar-bear effect and learn some super-easy ways that you and your family can reduce your footprint on the earth. Let's start keeping our planet happy, 'cause it's the only one we've got!

Giving Gal

"My family and I sponsored a little girl from Africa. Each month we get pictures, letters and updates on her. Not only has it opened our eyes to what's going on in the rest of the world, but we have a new member of the family. As a graduation gift for me, my family and I are going to travel to Tanzania to meet her!"
—Stephanie, 17

"I contributed to my school's Christmas Coat Drive last year. I didn't think too much of it—that is, until I saw a homeless women in my jacket. I couldn't believe that one small thing could make such a big difference in somebody's life. Now, I make sure I donate tons of stuff all year round. It's cool to know I can actually make a difference!"
—Laura, 15

"My parents give 10 percent of their income to our church. At first, I was kind of upset because that's a lot of money [to give away], especially for our family because we don't have much. But I realized that I'm really lucky to have everything I do, and that money goes to help people who need it more than us. Now, I give 10 percent of the money I make to our church, too. It's not much, but it's a start!"
—Rosa, 16

This is one of my favorite lessons in the book. Sure, confidence, body image, and relationships are super-important, too, but unless you feel you matter on a global scale, none of those other things will matter. There is no better way to feel a sense of worth than by giving back, whether you give of your time, money, or creativity. Giving will change the world, and it all starts with you.

If you don't give back and reinvest what you have been given, you will never feel satisfied, truly happy, or see your greater purpose. Having nice cars, purses, shoes, a dream house, a job, a man, and a bank account are all things you should strive for. There is no shame in wanting the toys, but if you hoard it all for yourself, your life will be incomplete. Giving back is the true key to happiness.

Here is what Bill Gates, founder of the Bill and Melinda Gates Foundation, said at the Harvard Commencement Speech he gave on June 2, 2007:

> *"If you believe every life has equal value, it's revolting to learn that some lives are seen as worth saving and others are not. We said to ourselves, 'This can't be true. But if it is true, it deserves to be the priority of our giving.'"*

My company, EG Inc., was founded because I wanted to give back to girls in need, here in Canada, in the U. S,, and around the world. My motto was and continues to be "Every gal matters." The goal of EG Inc. is to raise and donate $101,000,000 and empower 101,000,000 girls and young women around the world.

Right now, young people have more power than ever to change the world, and it's a really great time to be alive. It doesn't matter who you are, where you are, or what you have. It doesn't matter if you are rich or if you are poor. You don't need to be famous, have friends in high places, or have thousands of dollars in the bank to give back, to help, to make a difference. You are a citizen of a global community that needs you, and every little bit helps. You can start today, right now, from exactly where you are. You only need the awareness that we are all connected, and that every life matters. You can change the world.

If you are a super-busy college student and can only give three hours a month, give those three hours. If you are a high school girl just trying to get by, and all you can give is five dollars a week, give those five dollars. If you are only able to talk to one person about one cause that's really important, start there. You will probably get so addicted to how great it feels that you'll spend less time doing other things and more time giving. Just don't let the amount that you can give determine whether or not you will give.

Turn your passion into action, bit by tiny bit. Do it without a platform; do it on the tiniest scale, because giving is giving is giving. And every single drop of knowledge you have can spread. Every penny you can send to someone who needs it, every pair of eyes you open, matters.

Who Can Give

Anybody can give. You don't need to have an abundance of money, be a celebrity, or be driven only to dedicate your life to the service to others. If you are, kudos to you, but it's really not necessary. All you need to give back is a desire to make a difference, and I'm sure you're the kind of girl who wants to do what she can to help others.

All the "givers" you hear about on TV are the celebs who give the mega-money, adopt a fleet of kids (which is super-cool), or attend benefit events where they bid on awesome things and give the money to charity. Neither you nor I are in a position to do that right now, but our voice and actions count. There are thousands of causes and thousands of ways to help. Pick one, and do what you can. Not sure why you should give? I mean, you are just one person; how much could you actually do? Right? Wrong! You are way more powerful than you think and can do so much!

Top Ten Reasons to Volunteer and Give Back

1. To feel better about yourself. No matter how bad things are, if you reach out and help others, you won't be able to feel anything but amazing.
2. Find out what you love doing. If you are interested in a certain field, volunteering in it is a great way to see if you could do it for a living.
3. Have fun with your friends. Doing something really powerful with your friends will bring you closer together and be a ton of fun!
4. Fulfill graduation requirements. Most schools require a certain amount of volunteer time for you to graduate. (I did mine at a no-kill cat shelter, and I also worked with super-young teen moms.)
5. It looks great on a résumé or college application. You will gain a ton of self-esteem by getting out there and helping people, but it might just open doors for you, too.
6. To change lives and inspire others. It doesn't take much to touch somebody and change a life, and there is no better feeling in the world.
7. Learn important skills and find what you are interested in. Depending on what you are doing, you'll be picking up a wide variety of skills that you can use at work, at school, and in your life.
8. To get involved in your community and meet new people. Coming together as a group and making a difference for the people in your town or community and seeing the results will make you feel so proud of yourself.

9. Open your eyes about the world around you. Getting involved in a cause will put everything in perspective, and you will start seeing what's really important.
10. Because you can. There is something you can do every day to make the world a better place, even if it's a small thing. Small counts; everything counts. Do something every day.

For more info on volunteering, check out www.dosomething.org.

Important Causes

There are so many amazing causes in the world that need you to come on board and help them out. Here are just a few that are especially close to my own heart:

• Women's rights and issues. Millions of women have their human rights violated every single day. In the Democratic Republic of the Congo, Afghanistan, Rwanda, Kosovo, Sierra Leone, and Darfur, women are brutally raped on a daily basis as a weapon designed to destroy their families and futures. In Pakistan, the Middle East, Peru, Russia, and South Africa, women are beaten and killed for anything from suspected infidelity to making eye contact. Females in Thailand, Ukraine, and Burma are sold into the sex trade, some as young as six or seven years old, where they endure countless years of mental and physical abuse. Even here in North America, women face difficulty entering the workforce due to their reproductive status, and gay, lesbian, bisexual, and transgender youth are subject to exclusion, abuse, and violence.

• HIV/AIDS. The number of people living with HIV or AIDS right now has reached 38.6 billion. Of the 3.3 million people who died of AIDS in 2005 alone, 570,000 were children. The illness is spreading due to lack of education, ignorance, and the inability to access protection, and countless people are dying due the lack on antiretroviral medication that helps stop the disease's progress and helps the patient live a longer, more productive life. It is estimated that fifteen million children worldwide have been orphaned by the AIDS epidemic. It only costs a couple of dollars a month to provide the medicine needed to save lives.

• Education. One-third of all children never see the inside of a classroom. Fifty-seven percent of the over one hundred million children who don't get an education are girls. Of the 781 million people in the world who are illiterate, 64% are women. Many societies and cultures put more importance on boys getting an education, and the little girls are forced to stay home and help their mothers. Good news: It will only cost nine billion dollars to make sure every child in the world gets an education!

• Poverty. Over one billion people live on less than a dollar a day. This forces 250 million children between the ages of five and seventeen to work outside the home.

• Cruelty to animals. I think animals are the most amazing things on this planet, and we are supposed to take care of them, not exploit them.

• Child labor. UNICEF estimates that there are 218 million child laborers between ages five and seventeen, worldwide. Two of the most shocking forms of child labor include children forced to fight in wars and child prostitution.

• Domestic violence. Women are six times as likely as men to experience domestic abuse, and some estimates state that 30%–50% of women experience it in their lifetime.

Did any of those facts send a chill up your spine? If so, pick one cause, Google it, and look for ways to get involved. Even if you just print up all the info you find, gather some pics, and make a huge poster to share with your classmates, you'll be doing something. Bonus points for collecting spare change from classmates and donating it.

Teens Helping Teens

"A lot of people loan their face to a cause, which is great, but it doesn't do as much as getting out there and actually physically doing something."
—Hayden Panettiere

It may seem that given the state of the world, you are powerless to do something. Problems seem so big, and you seem so small. Teen girls, in the great world of philanthropy, are often overlooked on both the giving end and the receiving. If we stuck together and focused our tremendous effort, creativity, and talent to make a difference, we could do so much good. When young people do things, adults sit up and take action also. It all starts with you, baby.

Here are some fun ways to start making a difference today!

Organize a "Giving Back" party. Here's how you do it: Choose a cause, organization, or charity that you believe in. Invite some pals (a group of five to twenty-five) and have them bring something that will contribute to the cause, like clothing, school supplies, toys, etc. Package these items and send them to your chosen charity or organization. Put together a presentation, explain about the cause to your pals, and then have some fun, knowing you did something great to give back!

Do a dollar drive. Penny drives have raised millions of dollars, but I think we can do better. Teen girls spend billions of dollars a year on clothes, cosmetics, and things like iPods and laptops. I say collecting the loose dollar bills or coins isn't too much to ask. Set up collection tins (decorated super-cute … by you, of course) in different classrooms, at your gym, at your parents' workplaces, etc. Empty them out every week and send in the money to your cause. Alert the media, once you've got the ball rolling, to spread the word to get others involved.

Join in. There are so many runs, walks, or rides for the poor, the hungry, the sick, or the underprivileged. Sign up for one of these, and go door to door, raising money for it. Have your neighbors sponsor you, and donate the dough to the people in need.

Swap. You can't deny that you have loads of unused clothes and things in your room right now. I'm guilty of the same thing. So, why not give those clothes and things to somebody who really needs them. Invite your closest gal pals over and have them bring clothes they haven't worn in the last six months, stuff they have outgrown, or stuff that doesn't suit them anymore. They also should bring any loose change from around the house. Have them stop by your pad to wash and fold the clothes, and put them in boxes. Put the dough in an envelope and then go to your local women's shelter (most towns and cities have one) and drop the stuff off. And if it's allowed, see if you can spend some time getting to know the women and children. It will really open your eyes, and it will show the people in the shelter that they are cared about and that they do matter.

Put on a toy (coat, blanket, food) drive at your school. The great thing about being in school, and something I wish I had taken more advantage of when I was there, is the hundreds or thousands of people in close proximity. You have a built-in target market, and it's great for doing something big by getting everyone involved.

Sponsor a child. Remember those "for a dollar a day" or "for the price of a cup of coffee" ads? If you help one person get an education and pull himself or herself out of poverty, you will have done your part to literally change the world. Get your family involved and do it together. Bonus: It'll bring your family closer, too.

Visit www.thehungersite.com or www.freerice.com.
By clicking on the buttons, you will be donating money and food to people who need it most … and it doesn't cost you a thing. Cool, eh?

Collect old books. Illiteracy is one of the most terrible things in the world—it's so needless. Go door to door and ask your friends to donate old books for less fortunate kids and teens. Or ask the newspaper to write an article about your book drive, and ask readers to send in their old books also.

Daily acts of kindness. You don't have to be involved in a charity or organization to make a difference every day. You can do kind stuff for the people in your home or school. Here's how:

- Help the new kid clean up the contents of her pencil case if she drops it in the middle of the hallway.
- Invite the shy, quiet girl who doesn't have any friends to come and eat lunch with you and your friends.
- Make some dinners and freeze them in single servings to take to an elderly neighbor.
- Give a girl in your school your old prom dress if she can't afford one.
- Help an old lady reach the top shelf at the grocery shelf.
- Bake cookies for your study group.
- Photocopy your notes for a classmate who missed class.
- Buy flowers for a friend, family member, teacher, or co-worker, or send them to somebody in the hospital with an inspiring note attached.
- Treat a homeless person to lunch.
- Buy some baby clothes, formula, or toys, and take them down to an unwed mothers shelter.
- Pick up some nail polish, beauty products, hair products, or moisturizer, and drop it off at a battered women's shelter. (Even better if you and your friends offer to give the mani's and pedi's.)
- Weed your neighbor's garden.
- Dog (cat, fish, hamster) sit when a friend goes out of town.

Taking Your Cue from Well-Known Givers

If you still feel like you can't really make a difference, that's all about to change. The following people have given so much and made a huge difference, and there is no reason why you can't, too. Time to get inspired, ladies!

Oprah Winfrey. Again, my girl Oprah needs some kudos here. Her Angel Network has raised over fifty million dollars. She gave fifteen million of that to the victims of Hurricane Katrina, funded sixty schools in places like Africa and Asia, and gave forty million dollars of her own money to open a state-of-the-art Oprah Winfrey Leadership Academy in South Africa. How amazing is that? Look what one person can do! Just think about all the lives that the Angel Network will change and all the giving that will inspire.

Shakira. In 2007, Shakira founded the Pies Descalzos Foundation that provides schooling for poor children in Columbia. She is also a UNICEF Goodwill Ambassador; she was chosen, according to their executive director, "based on her compassion, her involvement in global issues, her deep commitment to helping children, and her appeal to young people around the world." Her latest charity, Latin America for Solidarity, has donated forty million dollars to victims of natural disasters, and donated five million dollars to four Latin American countries for education and health. We love Shakira!

Petra Nemcova. After she survived the 2004 tsunami that claimed the life of her fiancé, Petra founded the Happy Hearts Fund. Its mission is to help children who have suffered due to natural, economic, or health-related disasters. So far, they have established programs in Thailand, Indonesia, Sri Lanka, Pakistan, Indonesia, Cambodia, Vietnam, and Czech Republic.

Craig and Mark Kielburger. Craig and Mark, in their early twenties, are already child rights activists, leadership specialists, NY Times best-selling authors, and the founders of Free the Children, the world's largest network of kids helping kids. They have impacted well over one million young people around the world, have built over 450 elementary schools, and provide education to 40,000 kids every day! And the coolest part is, Craig was only fourteen when he founded Free the Children! Check them out at www.freethechildren.com. If they can do it, so can you!

Get involved in any one of these amazing organizations, or start your own! The bottom line is that we can be the generation that puts an end to poverty, child labor, and illiteracy, and we can leave a lasting legacy. You can have a huge impact on the world, and by getting your friends and their friends involved, there isn't anything we can't do. I believe that, completely, and if you do, too, please take the time to go to www.empoweredgal.com to find out how we can work together to make this planet a better place—for everybody.

Green Gal

"It doesn't take much to actually make a difference. I'm actually kind of surprised. Global warming seems like such a big deal, and it is, but really small things add up quickly and make such a huge difference. How can you not make the extra effort to save the planet?"

—Amber, 16

"I turn the lights off when I leave the room, carpool to school, ride my bike to my friend's house, and I recycle. I feel like I'm doing my part for the environment."

—Tiffany, 18

Unless you've been living under a rock, it's impossible that you haven't heard about global warming and the effects it's having on our planet and our future. Our planet is passed down from one generation to the next, and it's in our hands right now. We have a choice to either keep going the way we are going, or we, teen girls across the globe, can come together and do small things every day to improve the situation and leave Mother Earth a little better off than how we inherited it. After all, she is our main gal!

What IS Global Warming?

Global warming is caused by carbon dioxide (CO_2) and other gasses that trap solar heat in the atmosphere. A certain amount of that is good—it keeps the temperatures on the earth habitable. But because of the amount of fossil fuels that we burn, such as gas and oil, combined with the eradication of many of the world's forests (which convert CO_2 to oxygen), the temperature of our earth is on the rise.

It is happening all around us. The icecaps and glaciers are melting, animals near the North and South Poles are dying and having to find new habitats, and storms are on the rise. The average American, according to climatecrisis.com (where all these stats and facts come from), produces 7.5 tons of CO_2 emissions each year. I say we can do better!

If we don't do something about it:
- Over one million species could be extinct by 2050 (Yup, gals, that's in our lifetime!)

- The Arctic Ocean could be without ice by 2050.
- Heat waves will be common, as will droughts and fires
- Within twenty-five years, approximately 300,000 people will die each year due to the effects of global warming
- Sea levels could rise up to twenty feet, which means that many coastal areas (California, Florida, and New York) could be underwater.

What You Can Do

Each one of us contributes to global warming every single day! We heat our homes, take long showers, and drive to school, the mall, and to our friends' houses. We eat red meat and inorganic food. The good news is that it's super-easy to reduce our carbon dioxide emissions and lessen our footprints on the planet, every single day. Here's how:

Find Your Polar-Bear Effect. Did you see the amazing TV series, Planet Earth, where the polar bear keeps swimming and swimming with no land in sight, trying to find food, because global warming has caused all the ice—its usual hunting grounds—to melt? It made me so sad, and as I sat there watching it, with the heater on and lights blazing, I realized that I had something to do with that. I contributed to that animal's struggles, a gazillion miles away.

Now when I leave a room and don't switch off the light, I see that polar bear, and go back and turn off the light. When I'm about to drive to Starbucks instead of walking, I see the polar bear. I call it the polar-bear effect. After everything I read and saw about the effects of global warming, that beautiful white bear was the one that really got to me. So, what's your "polar bear"?

Figure out what your reasons are for taking better care of our planet; there are some simple things you can do at home, at school, and in your community. Some require the help of your parents, so show them this chapter, explain why it's important to you, and see if they will help you—and our planet. You can do the following simple steps every day to give our Mama Earth a break:

In Your World

- Take digital pictures instead of using traditional film. Here's why: Not only are they easier to share with your friends, but they don't use any of those nasty chemicals, and you can choose to print only the ones you truly love, so less waste.

- When it comes to prom or special events, why spend a ton of money on a brand-new dress when you could just as easily (and cheaply!) borrow an older sister's or friend's, or shop second-hand? Here's why: A ton of energy and materials go into making all those dresses that are doomed for a life stuffed in the back of a closet.
- Use reusable mugs for your daily java jolt. Here's why: Because they are reusable, less junk ends up in our landfills, and less energy is required to make more.
- Instead of buying greeting cards, send e-cards, or make your own cards using recycled paper. Here's why: Again, less paper in landfills and fewer trees killed.
- Use the same towel all week long. Here's why: Less laundry = less water used = happier planet!

More fun, random ways to be a green gal:

- Reuse gift bags instead of tossing them.
- Use your own reusable bag when you go shopping. Find super-cute ones at www.reusablebags.com.
- Print school reports and papers on both sides to save paper.
- Recycle your old magazines. (Hint: If you want to keep your favorite articles, cut them out, stick them in a binder, and recycle the rest.)
- Get a reusable water bottle to get all the H2O you need.
- Have dinner by candlelight once a week. It could turn into a fun family tradition!
- Go to www.localharvest.com to find organic food stores in your area.
- Skip the one-time use things, like disposable razors, paper towels, plastic utensils, and the like. Invest in reusable items and keep our landfills cleaner.

At Home

Get your family involved and educate them on what's going on in the world and how they can help.

- Replace all your regular light bulbs with a compact fluorescent light bulb (CFL). Here's why: CFLs use 60 percent less energy than a regular bulb! That means that if you switched to them, you'll save about three hundred pounds of carbon dioxide every year. Get your friends to do it, too: If every family in the U.S. made the switch, we'd reduce carbon dioxide by more than ninety billion pounds.

- Only move your thermostat up two degrees in the winter and down two degrees in the summer. Here's why: Over half of the energy that is used in our homes is on heating and cooling. If you make the change, you'd save over two thousand pounds of carbon dioxide each year.
- Clean and replace furnace filters (or get your dad to do it!). Here's why: It'll save about 350 pounds of carbon dioxide each year!
- Look for the ENERGY STAR label when you buy new appliances. Here's why: If each household in America upgraded to more energy-efficient appliances, we'd save 175 million tons of carbon dioxide emissions each year.
- Cool down your water. Here's why: It takes a ton of energy to heat water, so try washing your clothes in cold or warm water, waiting until you have a full load, or doing loads back to back to avoid reheating the water. Take shorter, cooler showers, and install a low-flow showerhead. You'll save 850 pounds of carbon dioxide a year.
- Air dry your clothes. Here's why: Hanging your clothes out to dry for six months of the year (weather permitting) saves about 700 pounds of CO_2 a year!
- Switch off or unplug electronic devices. Here's why: By turning off your TV, radio, or computer when you leave the room, you'll cut back on thousands of pounds of CO_2 a year. If everybody actually unplugged the device, we'd save eighteen million tons of emissions each year. Did you know that plugged-in devices account for 5 percent of total domestic energy consumption?
- Recycle. Here's why: If you recycled half of your household garbage, you'd save about 2400 tons of emissions each year. Check out www.earth911.com to find resources in your community.
- Swap clothes. Here's why: Way less energy is used when you recycle clothes instead of buying new. So, get your gals together and switch clothes!
- Go green with cosmetics and clothing. Tons of companies are making products and clothing with organic materials and recycled packaging. Here's why: They are good for you and use way less energy to produce. Plus, they don't litter our landfills for years to come; they are biodegradable!

In Your Community

- Plant a tree. Here's why: One tree will absorb—get this—one ton of carbon dioxide in its lifetime! How cool is that? Plus, the shade it provides will reduce your air-conditioning bill by up to 15 percent. Go to www.arborday.com to find info on planting trees in your community.

- Buy local food. Here's why: Did you know that the average American meal travels 1,200 miles to get to your table? If you buy local produce, meat, and grains, you'll be saving fuel. Plus, you'll be benefiting your community. Check out your local farmers market with your family.
- But fresh food. Here's why: Not only does it taste better and is better for you, it takes ten times less energy to produce.
- Buy organic. Here's why: It costs more money; I'm not gonna lie. But here's the thing—it's way better for you, tastes better, and it isn't covered in poisonous pesticides. If we only grew all our corn and soybean crops organically, we'd save 580 billion pounds of carbon dioxide! And yeah, I said b-b-b-billion!
- Eat less beef. Here's why: Methane, produced by cattle, is the second most significant greenhouse gas. Plus, you'll feel better!
- Walk, bike, or carpool. Here's why: If you cut back just ten miles of driving every week, you'd personally save about five hundred pounds of carbon dioxide a year! If you carpool only two days a week, to and from school or work, you'd save almost sixteen hundred pounds!

At Your School

Encourage your school to go green. Here's why: Think of the impact it would have if your school went green! Encourage them to switch to CFL light bulbs, turn lights off when nobody is in the room, use lower heat settings and less air conditioning, change heating and cooling filters, install energy-efficient appliances, and recycle! If money is the concern, suggest a coin drive to pay for the upgrades.

Visit www.greenissexy.org to get a brand-new green tip every day!

Gal to Gal

"A girl in my school lost her house in a fire. Everybody chipped in and raised money through bake sales, a Run for Carly, where people in the neighborhood sponsored us and donated money, and a penny drive. We raised almost ten thousand dollars and helped her and her family get back on their feet. It felt amazing to be a part of something like that. My advice is to keep your eyes open. There is always somebody who could use your help, even if it's just a shoulder to cry on."
—Joy, 16

"There are so many causes that are important. Pick one, and do what you can, every day, to help."
—Lissa, 14

"Just do whatever you can. You don't have to change the world in a day, just work toward it every day. If everybody did that, the world would be such a better place."
—Kendal, 14

"Create a compost pile in your yard or on your deck. It saves a ton of garbage, and it actually goes back into the earth."
—Sophia, 15

"My friends and I care a lot about the environment. We even put on a Save the Planet day at our school for Earth Day. It was really cool to get everybody involved, brainstorming and putting their differences aside to try to make a difference."
—Ann, 17

"We recycle like crazy in my house; my mom is kind of a fanatic about it. But it makes me feel really good; we are actually making a difference."
—Nicole, 17

Hey, it's okay to:

- Feel kind of overwhelmed. It's a big world with lots of problems, but by picking even one thing you believe in and helping one person, you are doing so much.
- Get mad about the injustices you see. Just turn that anger into action, and do something about it.
- Expect the best. I was warned that this chapter might discourage girls because they might not be able to do much. Hello! I know you can do so much, and together, we can change the world. I believe that with my whole heart, and I hope you do, too.

-Okay, looks like you made it, you EG Graduate! Turn the page for a debriefing, a whole lot of kudos, and some more fun stuff!

Wrap Up!

There you have it, ladies! I tried to have confetti explode out of the last page, but for some reason, I was unable to make it happen. Instead, I hope the feeling you have right now is enough of a celebration for you. Maybe you are a little relieved, now that you have the basic tools to survive—and thrive—on the teen-o-coaster. Maybe you are really pumped and motivated to start making changes in your life and working towards the you that you want to be. Or maybe you are a little overwhelmed, trying to figure out where you are going to start.

No matter what you are feeling, I want you to keep a couple things in mind: First, change takes time, so go easy on yourself, and enjoy the ride. You aren't going to have everything all figured out right away—you aren't supposed to. You are a teen, and it's a crazy, scary, awesome time. You are going to discover a ton more about yourself as time goes on, so give yourself permission to not have it all figured out just yet.

Second, don't try to do everything all at once. Doing one thing a day is enough. A total life makeover takes time, so here's what I suggest you do: There were probably one or two parts that especially jumped out at you. Maybe you highlighted them, or circled them, or just made a mental note to go back to them. Pick those couple things, and work on them first. Then, once you have them under control, pick a couple more things you want to work on, and so on. Do-able? Good!

And, here are some things I want you to remember as you take this book's lessons out into the real world with you. (Yup, you guessed it—some final tips!)

Have fun with it! This is your life, so it's up to you to not only make the destination rock but the journey, too. There's a famous saying about how life happens when we are busy making plans, so slow down and smell the lattes, girls! Right now matters, too. Even if your life isn't exactly like you want it, you can still make the best of it, and take comfort in knowing that your future is in your own hands.

Believe in your goals! They matter, and sometimes they will be the only things that keep you going. My goals were a lifesaver for me, and I've worked hard to reach them and realize my dreams. Never listen to anyone who tells you that your dreams are unreachable. Follow your heart and find your passion, and do whatever it takes (within reason!) to make them happen. You are the only thing that can stop you.

Be you! I hope one of the messages you get from this book is that there is nobody better to be than you. Wanting to be like other people is a waste of all the potential and power you have inside you. Instead of hiding yourself or changing yourself, let you—whatever and whoever that may be—shine.

Give yourself permission to make mistakes. Mistakes are inevitable, and I've certainly made my fair share. But it's not the mistake that matters; it's what you decide to do about them. So you screwed up? So what? Now you are one step closer to figuring out the right way to do it. No matter what, keep going and keep learning from your mistakes instead of being defeated by them. This is your chance to start over!

Be positive. The Saturday Night Live character Debbie Downer might be funny, but nobody likes her in real life! Try to see the positive in situations, no matter how big or small.

Be a grateful gal. Gratitude is my favorite word and feeling. I try to live in a state of gratitude and being happy for what I have and appreciating every moment.

Pass on the empowerment! You know that in-control feeling you have about your life right now? Pass that on to your friends and help them get their EG on! The one thing every gal looks beautiful in is empowerment, so share what you know and help out your sisters. You are now an EG ambassador!

Write your own script. Forget what everybody tells you that you should or shouldn't be, or what you should do, or what you should look like. It's up to you, so stay true to yourself. Be your own girl, and rock it!

Keep this book handy—remember it's your BFFF (best book friend forever), so don't be shy! Keep coming back to it every time you need a little pick-me-up boost of empowerment or just need to have a friend tell you it's all going to be okay.

So, there you go! But don't think this is the end of our relationship; there is a ton more to come! Go to www.empoweredgal.com to get in on all the fun, help us reach our goal of raising all that money for gals in need, and get involved! Share your stories, help us with upcoming projects, have me stop by your school and a ton more!

And keep in touch! Send me an e-mail at kate@empoweredgal. com. I read them all!

xoxo

Kate

Have me speak at your school!

Did you like the book? Have me speak at your high school. It's totally easy, and if you are responsible for getting me booked, I'll give you a gift basket filled with EG goodies! Show this book and my speaker package (downloadable from www.empoweredgal.com) to your teachers and principal, and ask them to give me a call. Or, send me an e-mail with the name and contact info of the principal at your school, and I'll give him or her a call.

Here is a brief outline of some of our most popular topics:

- LeaderGal Leadership Workshop: LeaderGal Leadership workshops provide girls, ages eleven to eighteen, with a hands-on and interactive leadership experience. Designed to give girls the tools they need to succeed, achieve, and lead at home, at school, in their communities, and in their lives. Covers self-esteem building, teamwork vs. competition, risk-taking, reaching goals and dreams, being a leader in your own life, and more!
- 10 Keys to School Success
- Mega-Goals and Dreams: Getting from where you are to where you want to be
- The High School/College Girl's Guide to Career Success
- Overcoming Mean Girls, Bullies, and Cyber Attacks
- Be a Self-Esteem Queen

Visit us online for my complete speaker packages for high school and college audiences. Read what people are saying, and find out about my no-hassle, 100-percent money-back satisfaction guarantee!

Ideal for:

- Assemblies

- Student Leadership Events/Conferences

- Honor Society Programs

- Back- to- School Events

- Career Day/Internship Programs

- Alcohol/Drug Awareness Programs

- Commencements and Graduations

- Summer Programs and Camps

Join Us Online!

EG is on MySpace, so stop by and friend-request me!

www.MySpace.com/EmpoweredGal

And find us on **Facebook** and **My Yearbook**, too!

Official Site: **www.empoweredgal.com**

Check it out for a ton of freebies, additional info mentioned in the book, some cool extras, and find out how to be an EG Ambassador at your school!

❀ Notes ❀

❀ Notes ❀

❀ Notes ❀

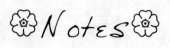

Notes

❀ Notes ❀

❀ Notes ❀

Printed in the United States
124992LV00003BA/130-408/P